HONEY, WE LOST THE KIDS:

Re-thinking Childhood in the Multimedia Age

HONEY, WE LOST THE KIDS:
Re-thinking Childhood in the Multimedia Age

Kathleen McDonnell

Second
Story
Press

NATIONAL LIBRARY OF CANADA
CANADIAN CATALOGUING IN PUBLICATION DATA

McDonnell, Kathleen, 1947–
Honey, we lost the kids: rethinking childhood in the multimedia age

Includes bibliographical references
ISBN 0-896764-37-1

1. Mass media and children. 2. Digital media — Social aspects. 3. Child
rearing.   I. Title.

HQ784.M3M32 2001   305.23   C2001-930248-7

Printed and bound in Canada

Edited by Judy MacDonald
Book Design and Cover ©2001 by Stephanie Martin
Author Photograph by Liz Dewdney

*Second Story Press gratefully acknowledges the support of the
Ontario Arts Council and the Canada Council for the Arts for our publishing program.
We acknowledge the financial support of the government of Canada through the
Book Publishing Industry Development program.*

Published by
SECOND STORY PRESS
*720 Bathurst Street, Suite 301
Toronto, Canada
M5S 2R4*
www.secondstorypress.on.ca

◆

Author's website: www.kathleenmcdonnell.com

Contents

ACKNOWLEDGEMENTS

I'M VERY GRATEFUL TO Maura McIntyre, Susan Roy and Alec Farquhar, who took the time to read the manuscript and gave me helpful criticism and insightful comments.

Judy MacDonald has been an excellent editor, giving me plenty of verbal pats on the back while constantly pushing me to clarify my thinking, back up my statements, and use more commas.

Margie Wolfe at Second Story Press has been a pillar of encouragement throughout my writing career, and I value her friendship and professionalism. I also want to say thank you to Liz Martin and Lois Pike for their support of my work over the years.

Many thanks for the funding assistance I received from both the Ontario Arts Council and the Canadian Studies Program, Department of Canadian Heritage, during the time I was researching and writing this book. Thanks also to Rick Salutin and Barry Duncan for their letters of support.

Without the love and encouragement of my partner Alec over the years (not to mention the fact that at least one of us has a steady income), I truly would not be able to do the work that I do.

I'm fortunate to have contact with a wide range of young people in my day-to-day life. I want to thank all my young friends — islanders and mainland-dwellers alike — for allowing me to poke my nose into their affairs, for answering my endless questions, and for making me laugh so often. I particularly want to acknowledge the contributions of my own children. Martha served as an unfailingly good-humored test case for many of the ideas in my earlier book, *Kid Culture*. With *Honey, We Lost the Kids* it's Ivy's turn, and she's been a spirited collaborator every step of the way. She's forthright in her opinions (to put it mildly) and never hesitates to tell me when I'm completely off-base. The contents of that wonderful brain continue to amaze and delight me.

INTRODUCTION

MADAME DE SADE'S HOUSE OF TOTAL DISCLOSURE

I T WAS MADAME DE SADE who brought it home to me that childhood as we know it had passed into history.

I was watching the six o'clock news with my younger daughter, Ivy, when an item came on about a woman's arrest for running a "common bawdy house" (that quaint legal term) in one of Toronto's northern suburbs. The place was no ordinary house of ill repute, however: it specialized in bondage and sadomasochism, and was known as Madame de Sade's House of Pain. The news item showed footage of Madame's "dungeon," replete with whips, chains, rubber suits and other paraphernalia to feed every fetish. There was my ten-year-old, sitting on the couch, taking it all in. (Not for nothing has television been called "the total disclosure medium.") Apparently Madame de Sade's defence was that her service shouldn't be considered prostitution, because what she was offering was a form of therapy rather than sex. "So it will be up to the courts to decide," the reporter intoned, "whether wrapping a chain around a penis constitutes sex."

In our house the kitchen, dining and living areas are all one (not-so-big) room, so watching TV is generally a group activity. We kibitz about the news together, howl at *The Simpsons* together and jeer at blatantly manipulative commercials together. But on this particular evening I — for one of the few times in my life — was rendered utterly speechless. I had absolutely no idea where to begin to explain what this news item was all about, no inkling of how to make it into what media educators call a "teachable moment."

To my great relief, I didn't have to say anything. It was abundantly clear that this was one of those occasions when Ivy didn't *want* me to say anything, that this information fell squarely in the category of icky stuff that she didn't really want to know about yet, and that when the time came, she'd much rather find out about it in the neutral zone of grade five puberty class than from her mom. (Though I very much doubt a seminar about wrapping penises in chains will be taught in puberty class anytime soon.) As it turned out, my discomfort was just a taste of what was to come later that year, when millions of parents squirmed in embarrassment as their kids got a short course in the mechanics of oral sex on the nightly news during the Clinton sex scandal. Television, as Neil Postman observes in *Building a Bridge to the Eighteenth Century,* "does not segregate its audience ... it communicates the same information to everyone, simultaneously, regardless of age, sex, level of education." [1]

Or, to put it another way: our kids are all growing up in Madame de Sade's House of Total Disclosure.

It wasn't always so, of course. Once upon a time, kids grew up in well-defined stages, and it was the job of adults to implement a commonly agreed-upon schedule of maturity, to shield children from certain matters until they were "ready" to learn about them. Of course, kids themselves usually had other plans ...

I'm ten years old, paging through our household dictionary. Something I do a lot of these days. What was that word that older girl whispered on the playground today when Sister Nazarius' back was turned? Something like "fuck-er"? I search and search but all I can find is "fokker," which is the name of some kind of Second World War German fighter plane. Could that be it? As insults go, it seems pretty tame ...

What about that other word? I keep hearing other kids say it, and I pretend I know what they're talking about. No matter how many times I look, all I can find is one word: "hoar" meaning "grey" or "frosty." That can't be it. How else can you spell a word that sounds like "hore"?

I know this much: both those words have something to do with that THING that grown-ups know about, that THING they're keeping from me …

I'm gonna find out what those words mean if it kills me …

When I think about the enormous shift that's taken place in North America around sex and language since my childhood, I feel like some old codger marveling at how things change in a lifetime: *"Back when I was young we combed through the dictionary looking for dirty words, and most of 'em weren't even there. You kids nowadays can find out everything you need to know from an Eminem video or an episode of* Friends!" No doubt about it: childhood ain't what it used to be. The traditional schedule of maturity has been tossed out the window.

Honey, we lost the kids. They've grown up without having a chance to *be* kids.

But unlike the bumbling scientist in the popular Disney comedy who finally figures out how to restore his kids to normal after he accidentally shrinks them down to microscopic size, it doesn't look like we have a hope in hell of giving our kids a "real" childhood. Not a good old-fashioned one. Not anymore.

Over the past few decades, the lament that kids in our culture are growing up too fast has been raised by a mounting chorus of voices. One of the earliest and most influential was psychologist David Elkind, who popularized the phrase in the subtitle of his 1981 book, *The Hurried Child: Growing Up Too Fast Too Soon.* Elkind warns that modern parents are subjecting kids to what he calls "force blooming," or putting unprecedented pressure on them to excel instead of letting them mature at a normal pace. Elkind's warnings resound even more strongly now, as the media bombard us with images of parents drilling pre-schoolers with flash cards and fast-tracking seven-year-olds into computer camps. *The Hurried Child* focuses on social pressure for children to be high achievers, but a couple of years later, author Marie Winn added TV to the list of damaging influences on the young. In *Children without Childhood,* Winn argues that by exposing kids to a harsh and violent world, television is responsible for the destruction of what she calls the "protective membrane that once served to shelter children from precocious experience and sorrowful knowledge of the adult world." [2]

The concerns raised by Elkind and Winn in the early eighties were cited with growing frequency throughout the next two decades. Two of the most sensational media stories of the mid-nineties provided fodder for the growing sentiment that kids were being robbed of childhood. In 1996, Jessica Dubroff's attempt to become the world's youngest cross-country pilot ended in death for the seven-year-old, her father, Lloyd, and her flight instructor. Their single-engine Cessna took off in rain and high winds, only to plummet into a Cheyenne, Wyoming residential neighborhood minutes later. Jessica's mother, Lisa Hathaway, defended the decision to allow the child to fly. "Jessica died doing what she loved," *People* magazine quoted her as saying at the funeral. But the reaction of an outraged public was to ask what the hell a seven-year-old was doing at the controls of an airplane in the first place. The following year, six-year-old JonBenet Ramsey, a child beauty pageant winner, was found murdered in her home in an upscale Boulder, Colorado neighborhood. The child's parents were the subjects of what was generally agreed to be a bungled investigation by local police. More than four years later, no one has ever been charged with the murder. The media whirl surrounding these two tragic incidents was further heightened by the fact that both girls were engaged in activities that, in the eyes of most people, were completely inappropriate for children their age.

The solution, in the minds of some, is to try and turn back the clock. *Saving Childhood: Protecting our Children from the National Assault on Innocence,* by the husband-and-wife team of film critic Michael Medved and psychologist Diane Medved, is in this vein. The powerful lure of nostalgia for childhood the way it used to be (or at least, the way many people would like to think it was) pervades this 1998 book. But though the Medveds essentially recycle and re-cast the arguments of previous writers on childhood, the tone of their book is a distinct departure from the well-reasoned polemics of the likes of Elkind and Winn. *Saving Childhood* is, at its core, a rant against modern life, in which the Medveds trot out a by-now-famil-iar litany of complaints: that kids today are growing up socially, psy-chologically and intellectually impoverished; that they don't have a "real" childhood; that they're foul-mouthed, media-besotted couch potatoes who don't respect their elders. It's a view typified by this rather cranky outburst from the book:

> When was the last time you saw a child rise when an older person entered the room? When was the last time you saw children wait to be served food until the grown-ups got their share? When, indeed, have you run across kids who address adults they meet as Mr. or Mrs.? More likely, when parents introduce a business associate, kids grunt; when riding on a bus, they sit right where they are and look away when a senior citizen hobbles aboard. Generally, kids think nothing of criticizing their parents to their friends, or peppering their speech with expletives. [3]

Saving Childhood is full of these kinds of unexamined assump-tions about good behavior in childhood. Why should children stand when an adult enters the room? Because that's the way things have "always" been done. Why should they refrain from helping them-selves until all the adults at the table have been served? (This reminds me of the practice, in some cultures, where women don't eat until the men have had their fill.) Why shouldn't they feel free to criticize their parents? What if their complaints are legitimate and they need someone to confide in? Because we tell them not to air their dirty linen in public. In the Medveds' scheme of things, tradi-tional (that is, mid-Victorian) child-rearing practices have somehow taken on the patina of eternal verities.

In one particularly telling incident, the Medveds recount the mini-crisis that ensued in their household when their seven-year-old daughter, Sarah, brought home Judy Blume's enduringly popular novel *Are You There God? It's Me, Margaret* on the recommendation of a local librarian. Published in 1970, the book deals with eleven-year-old Margaret's spiritual quest to understand the workings of God in her own life — more specifically, why He hasn't arranged for her to get her first period yet when all her friends have gotten theirs. Since Sarah was clearly a bright child, reading well above her age level, the librarian presumably thought she'd respond to — and that her devoutly Jewish parents would approve of — Margaret's grappling with her faith and Jewish identity, subjects that are at the book's core. The Medveds, however, were distressed when, one night at the dinner table, Sarah piped up, "What's all this about girls and blood?" Instead of answering the child's question in a way appropriate for her age, they took the book away on the spot, telling her, "It's nothing you have to worry about right now, honey." And, to avoid future problems, they adopted a curious "protective policy" for their daughter's library visits:

> Before she checks out a book ... she'll look at the copyright date to make sure it was written before 1960. We've discovered the hard way that work from these earlier days can usually be better trusted to portray childhood the way Sarah feels it should be — with issues and problems of the sort girls typically and appropriately confront: who will be friends with whom, how to earn spending money, mastering a two-wheeler, or planning a surprise birthday party. In Sarah's unsophisticated world, teachers and parents are authorities, little brothers are pests, and girlfriends are accomplices ... For her, ignorance is cherished bliss. [4]

Few parents are prepared to go as far in their protective efforts as forbidding kids to read books written after 1960. But the Medveds give voice to a widespread sentiment, and the message of *Saving Childhood* has a powerful appeal in these confusing times. It's understandable that people would want to hark back to that pre–sixties *Leave it to Beaver* era when adults were adults, kids were kids and everybody knew their place. As we enter the 21st century, most of our ideas about childhood are stuck back in the 19th.

* * *

In *Saving Childhood,* Michael and Diane Medved come across as concerned, caring parents whose kids are the center of their universe — just like mine are for me. In truth, we're not all that different. But where they disown the world their kids are growing up in, I embrace it. Where they think things are getting irrevocably worse for children, I believe in many ways things are getting better.

How did we arrive at such different conclusions?

Like the Medveds, I'm a member of the baby-boom generation. (In their book, Michael makes much of his sixties' youth. But, while it's not impossible to picture him in long hair and love beads, I think his counter-cultural credentials were mostly sartorial, as they were for a lot of hippies.) My ideas here are very much the product of my own experiences as a parent, which have played out right in the thick of the heated debates that have raged in recent decades.

Both my daughters were born at home, caught by their father, Alec, with the assistance of midwives. (In Ivy's case, she came into the world so quickly that the midwife didn't make it in time.) They were breast-fed, diapered in reusable cloth (and yes, the occasional disposable), and later fed vegetables that we pureed ourselves rather than baby food from a jar. We sent them to cooperatively run day-cares, and gave them permission to call us by our first names. (This lasted until the day Martha, our firstborn, let it be known that she'd really rather call us "mom" and "dad.") Yes, we did it all, with a few exceptions — because of my insomniac tendencies, I had to draw the line at the family bed. But overall, I've been pretty much a textbook example of my generation's quest to reinvent the art of parenting, to be guided by more flexible, "child-led" principles than the ones we were raised on.

Soon after Martha was born, we moved to Ward's Island, a fifteen-minute ferry ride from downtown Toronto. It's a real, functioning community, where kids grow up surrounded by people who've known them from birth, where the lines separating family from not-family are pretty fluid and where the bonds of responsibility and affection are in no way confined to biological relations. Living on the island has been invaluable to me in writing this book, because it's given me the opportunity to watch boys and girls grow up together over the years, an experience that's increasingly rare in urban society. On our safe and relatively car-free island, kids have a world of their own, away from constant adult supervision. At the same time — somewhat paradoxically — our children become part of the community from the day they're born. They sleep in baby strollers at dances in the community hall, and participate in festivals, events and even the community Talent Show, right alongside the adults. Ever since Hillary Rodham Clinton borrowed the African saying "It takes a village to raise a child" for the title of her 1996 book, the phrase has become something of a contemporary cliché. But where I live, it's a tangible reality: the island community has played as important a role in "raising" my kids as Alec and I have. We think our kids are fortunate to be growing up in a larger world, with broader influences and wider possibilities than we could ever give them through our parenting abilities alone. It's a stream that flows both ways: living on the island, I've played a large part in "raising" a number of kids who aren't related to me biologically, but who I regard as family nonetheless. These experiences have been key to shaping my ideas on parenting and the importance of community.

I wasn't always so sanguine about those outside influences. Like many people of my generation, when I first became a parent I resolved that my household would be a protective haven from all the sexism, consumerism and other evils of modern life. But my daughters had other ideas. They wanted to play with Barbies, wear make-up, do all those girlie things. I wanted to shut out that pop-culture panorama, that batteries-sold-separately world, but they were determined to grow up *in* it. Other parents I knew were wrestling with the same dilemmas with sons who clamored for war toys and who imitated the cool martial-arts moves they had seen on *Teenage Mutant Ninja Turtles* and *Mighty Morphin Power Rangers.* My earlier book, *Kid Culture,* published in 1994, is largely the product of watching Martha and her friends grow up through the eighties and early nineties. It is also a chronicle of the parenting controversies that were getting a lot of media play during that time. I came around to the view that pop culture wasn't the demonic force it was cracked up to be. The central argument of *Kid Culture* is that adults have to stop censoring and raging against all the things kids like, and instead try to understand the powerful appeal that these toys, films, TV shows and video games have for them.

Watching my second child grow up has, in many ways, been quite a different story. Ivy was born in 1988, just as the demographic "echo" of baby-boomer offspring was cresting. In the intervening years between my two daughters, the landscape of childhood changed so much that many of those debates in the early nineties began to seem almost quaint. Forget Barbie, Power Rangers and other fantasy characters: by the late nineties, little boys were idolizing real-life wrestlers like Stone Cold Steve Austin, while girls as young as four were dressing up in tight skirts and platform shoes like Posh Spice. There are other ways in which my kids' childhoods have played out very differently. Having grown up with computers, for instance, Ivy is far more tech-savvy than her older sister. And from the age of nine or ten she was infinitely more aware of brands and labels — things Martha had only the vaguest clue about at that age. Ivy also knows far more about money, has seen more "adult" movies and is generally more knowledgeable about the larger world. Martha herself has commented that her little sister is much more worldly than she was at the same age. So the popular belief has a lot of truth in it: kids really *are* growing up faster than ever. And to a large extent, this book is a chronicle of that accelerated rate of change in the landscape of childhood, which I've been able to observe from a front-row seat right in my own home.

Like the Medveds, many parents are reacting to these changes by reverting to old-style parenting and traditional discipline. For baby-boomer parents, this tendency seems to kick in when their kids hit puberty. It's as if many of us have been seized by a kind of collective amnesia about our own youthful rebellions, declaring instead that — to paraphrase the hymn about that old-time religion — "It was good enough for my father, and it's good enough for me." It's part of the nostalgia for the simpler times of the fifties. The problem is, a lot of that nostalgia is based on half-truths, wishful thinking and outright lies. There was indeed a much-vaunted "social consensus" in the fifties. But it was experienced by many people who lived through the period as stultifying, straightjacketed conformity. The fifties were a very comfortable time for those who fit the prevailing definition of normality. But it was also a time when kids were beaten with straps by their teachers, husbands could hit their wives with relative impunity and child sex abuse was a dirty family secret. It was also a terrible time for children and adults who were considered different, who in some cases lived in terror because they didn't fit in.

I grew up in the good old days. You can have them.

* * *

"Tide lets kids be kids." "Chuck E. Cheese's, where a kid can be a kid." These commercial jingles play on some popular and well-entrenched sentiments about childhood: that it's the time of life when human beings should be free to get dirty, eat junk food and generally run amok (as long as the good folks at Chuck E. Cheese's will clean up after them). But when you really think about them, these slogans also lead to some deeper questions: What is childhood? What is the experience of *being* a child, as opposed to what adults *think* about it? What I hope to do here is take out and examine some of our culture's most tenacious and deeply held assumptions about children and childhood, to see how they stack up against what's really going on in kids' lives now. The questions at the heart of this book are: How are the idea of childhood and the experience of being a child changing? How should adults respond to these changes?

The experience and information I draw on for this book come from the milieu I live in and know first-hand: that of kids growing up in Canada, the United States and other industrialized nations, who have ample access to media and consumer goods. In poorer nations, and in societies where the extended family is still the norm, children's lives are very different. In many parts of the world, where people are coping with the ravages of war, poverty and natural disasters, there's a bitter irony in even talking about a protected realm of childhood. Nevertheless, the changes that are happening in childhood in the developed countries do have an impact on these societies, also. Kids can watch *The Simpsons* in Hindi and they pack stadiums in the Philippines to see Britney Spears. It's increasingly clear that they're growing up in a global culture, sharing the same pop culture icons, coveting the same consumer goods.

At the beginning of this chapter I spoke of the yawning gap between my daughter Ivy's experience of growing up and my own repressed, fifties-era childhood. But the contrast doesn't only lie in *what* we were exposed to, but in our responses to it: I *wanted* to know about the hidden things. I tried my best to find out what they were, but no one would tell me. Ivy, on the other hand, finds out plenty without even having to ask. Often things are thrust in her face — like Madame de Sade's House of Pain — that she doesn't *want* to know about, at least not yet. What she *doesn't* have is that sense of secrets, of dark, forbidden corners, of wide swaths of knowledge being withheld from her — things that marked my growing-up years so strongly. Which is better? Which is worse? Who can say? Like most things in life, it's a trade-off. Personally, I'm far from convinced that I had it better growing up in the fifties than Ivy does in this turbulent new millennium.

Most adults try to block out the untidy emotions and realities of being a child. They honestly believe, like the Medveds, that kids desire nothing more than to dwell in a Land of Bland where "ignorance is cherished bliss," where their emotions run the gamut from nice to not-so-nice. But childhood has its terrors, its dark corners — always has, always will. Much as we want to do what we can to protect children from the pain of living, I don't think we do them any favors when we try to deny the existence of those dark corners altogether.

We think that if only we can slap enough Parental Advisory stickers on all those profanity-laced hip-hop CDs, if only we can make a V-chip that's powerful enough or an Internet filtering program sophisticated enough, then we can rebuild that protective membrane around childhood and set things right again. But it won't happen. The deck has been re-shuffled. Everything about childhood — and about children's relationship to the realm of adulthood — is undergoing profound change. As the words of the old Mother Goose rhyme go: "All the king's horses and all the king's men couldn't put Humpty Dumpty together again." In this case it's the wall we've erected around childhood that can't be put back together. But, like the poor, misguided king's men, we keep on trying to do just that.

Why do we do it? I think it stems from a frantic but misguided effort to relieve our own anxieties about the future. The truth is, kids are growing up in a very different world than we did. Instead of disowning it, what we should be doing is helping them learn to navigate it, a theme I'll be returning to throughout this book. What's happening is a profound and (I believe) inexorable historical shift in our culture, in which children are experiencing life beyond the protected but constricting confines of parental influence much earlier than they have for the past few centuries. After what we call the toddler stage, children are becoming participants in the larger society beyond the family: as they did for much of Western history; as they still do today in many traditional tribal societies. But it's scary for us to surrender them to the culture, to give up that control, to stop thinking of kids as our personal creations, and see them as members of the community at large. It goes completely against the notions of individualism and the privacy of family life that have prevailed here for the past few hundred years, which have led us to over-emphasize parenting at the expense of the communal responsibilities for child rearing.

Why, it needs to be asked, have so few adults seriously considered the possibility that there might be positive aspects to the demise of traditional childhood? As much as we'd prefer to cling to the belief that things are always getting worse — that the world's going to hell in a handbasket — maybe we should consider a truly novel, even radical idea: that things may be getting better for kids.

Have we really "lost" the kids? No. Despite all the jeremiads and media hype, kids are still kids — biologically, developmentally, psychologically. What we are losing, though, is the old *idea* of childhood, which is largely a set of assumptions that don't match up with contemporary realities — new technologies and mass media, fallen taboos, changing family structures and the growing recognition of the rights of children.

NOTES

1. Neil Postman, *Building a Bridge to the Eighteenth Century: How the Past Can Improve Our Future* (New York: Alfred A. Knopf, 1999), 192.
2. Marie Winn, *Children Without Childhood* (New York: Pantheon Books, 1983), 4.
3. Michael Medved and Diane Medved, *Saving Childhood: Protecting Our Children from the National Assault on Innocence* (New York: Harper Collins, 1998), 11.
4. Ibid., 13.

THE WALLED GARDEN OF CHILDHOOD

"CHILDHOOD IS NOT A BIOLOGICAL NECESSITY but a social construction."[1] That's a rather startling statement from the esteemed social critic Neil Postman, one that on the face of it seems patently untrue. Childhood is a fundamental and universal condition of human existence; it begins at birth and continues as children grow in size, learn to walk and talk and develop specific motor and cognitive skills. "Not a biological necessity"? As the kids themselves might say: *Oh, puh-leeze!*

But children — living, breathing biological creatures — and childhood are not the same things. What Postman is getting at here is the *idea* of childhood — the set of beliefs, and the values attached to it. When he calls it a social construction, he means the way we *think* about childhood, as distinct from children themselves. It's the evolution of this idea that I want to explore in this chapter, a process that I think is crucial to understanding what's happening to childhood today. The present Western view of childhood is based on a number of assumptions that are far from universal in human societies, and that developed fairly recently even in our own history. Childhood as we think of it is a modern invention. Through most of human history, childhood didn't exist as a separate sphere of life. It's urban industrialized society that is the historical blip, the great exception.

14

The Invention of Childhood

In 1962, French historian Philippe Ariès published *Centuries of Childhood,* his seminal work on the history of childhood in Western culture. Ariès' chief — and still controversial — argument is that, "in medieval society, the idea of childhood did not exist," that the modern distinction between children and adults only gradually emerged over the subsequent centuries. Ariès traces the evolution of childhood through the depictions of children in the art of various historical periods, the appearance of a distinct style of dress for children and the rise of the modern system of universal education. How is it possible to speak of inventing something as natural as childhood? It was Ariès who first posed the idea that childhood is not simply a biological phenomenon but also an invention of human culture. What concerns him in *Centuries of Childhood* is the evolution of the idea of childhood through various historical periods and cultural contexts.

To understand something of what the experience of childhood was like in medieval times, we have to imagine ourselves in a society in which most children, once they are old enough to walk, talk and perform tasks, are totally integrated into community life. There was no concept of universal education as we understand it today. While there were schools in the Middle Ages, they existed chiefly to educate the sons of the nobility. The children of the peasantry labored in the fields alongside their parents and older siblings. They performed domestic tasks and worked as apprentices to craftsmen at very young ages. In play as well as work, there were no sharp distinctions between the generations. In industrialized countries we accept as a given that children and adults enjoy separate and distinct forms of entertainment, but this wasn't true of the medieval world, where people of all ages took part in the great seasonal festivals — dancing, making music, joining in pageants, listening to itinerant storytellers, playing Ring-around-the-Rosy and hand-clapping games. The sorts of amusements that many now regard as childish were indulged in by young and old alike. Though children played with simple toys like rattles, blocks and balls, the idea of a whole class of objects and whole areas of behavior consigned to one age group was completely foreign to the medieval mind. As Ariès puts it, medieval society "made no distinction between children and adults, in dress or in work or in play."[2]

Other historians have taken exception to some of Ariès' ideas, particularly the notion that parents in the Middle Ages lacked what we would regard as the normal feelings of interest in and affection for their children. In her book *Childhood in the Middle Ages,* published in 1990, historian Shulamith Shahar points out that medieval child care was in many ways similar to current "child-centered" practices. Mothers breast-fed their babies on demand (the practice of sending infants out to wet-nurses was not to become widespread until a couple of centuries later). Small children were frequently allowed to run naked. Discipline was fairly relaxed or, as it would probably be called today, "permissive." But Ariès himself makes a crucial distinction between feelings toward individual children and the collective consciousness around childhood itself:

> This is not to suggest that children were neglected, forsaken or despised. The idea of childhood is not to be confused with affection for children: it corresponds to an awareness of the particular nature of childhood, that particular nature which distinguishes the child from the adult, even the young adult. In medieval society this awareness was lacking.[3]

But sentiments toward very young children were undeniably colored by the high rate of infant mortality in the medieval world. Many babies died at birth or soon after, and many more succumbed to disease in the first few years of life. What might appear as callousness or indifference toward the very young was, in Ariès' view, "a direct and inevitable consequence of the demography of the period. People could not allow themselves to become too attached to something that was regarded as a probable loss." [4] Reinforcing his view is the fact that, up until the 17th century, stillborn babies and infants who died soon after birth were not given names, and were buried in unmarked graves. Though today we regard it as a given that children become full members of the family at birth, this was not the case throughout much of the past. The simple fact of having been born was not enough to qualify a child for membership in the family or in the larger society, or even to ensure its survival. This is apparent from the widespread practice of child abandonment or exposure, a phenomenon that has occurred in all periods of Western history, but that has rarely been written or talked about.

Historian John Boswell documents this hidden history of childhood in his 1988 book, *The Kindness of Strangers*. The reasons for child abandonment, Boswell notes, were complex and varied, having to do with factors such as poverty and sex roles. Female babies, who would eventually grow up and require dowries to be married off, were considered more expendable than males, for example. Though moral qualms about the practice date back to ancient times and the Catholic Church formally condemned it in the 13th century, there is no doubt that the exposure of infants was widely practiced in the medieval period and during the subsequent centuries. People viewed it as a method of family limitation, a necessary evil in order to ensure their own economic survival, and they frequently ignored the church's moral censure (not unlike many Catholics do today with abortion and birth control). Taking these realities into account, it's probably more accurate to say that medieval parents did develop bonds of affection with those children whom they chose to keep and rear, and who were lucky enough to survive infancy. It's important to note, too, that abandonment is far from unknown here and now, as we know from news reports that appear with regularity about babies disposed of in washrooms, trash cans and dumpsters. And, echoing the practice of "potting" infants in public places in the ancient world, there have been reports from Europe and Africa of so-called baby mailboxes: repositories monitored by child welfare authorities where parents can anonymously leave unwanted infants to be put up for adoption.

Though other historians take issue with some of the particulars of Ariès' argument, most agree with his basic contention that the medieval world did not have the strict separation of child and adult realms that developed in later centuries. In this sense, *Centuries of Childhood* defined the territory for the modern view of childhood and laid the groundwork for subsequent commentators. For example, in his influential 1982 book, *The Disappearance of Childhood,* Neil Postman elaborates on Ariès' main thesis and goes on to argue that not only is modern childhood a social construction, but it was created by the invention of the printing press and the subsequent rise in literacy throughout the Western world.

In the medieval world, there were no taboos: all aspects of life were within the purview of children, and little was withheld from them. Since children were so thoroughly integrated into everyday life, they were routinely exposed to adult behavior that many people today would consider unsuitable, including drunkenness and bawdy language. They would also witness death as a fact of life, since there were no hospitals and the mortally ill died at home in their beds. Family members slept in the same rooms, often in the same beds, and children were only haphazardly shielded from adults' sexual behavior. In fact, everybody did everything — visit, eat, work, play, sleep — in large common areas. (Today we'd say those medieval folks had lots of "boundary issues.")

Postman maintains that the invention of the printing press and the subsequent spread of literacy made possible the notion that children should inhabit a separate realm of life, one in which they're kept ignorant of what he calls "cultural secrets" — areas of knowledge pertaining, in large part, to sexuality. Widespread literacy makes the keeping of these cultural secrets possible, because it creates two classes of people: those who can read and those who can't. Postman argues that, in a largely non-literate culture, knowledge is transmitted by visual images and by speech, and is thus accessible to everyone except infants. But in literate cultures, a good deal of knowledge is communicated via written language, and can only be decoded by those who can read. In the medieval world, of course, very few adults could read, so everyone was privy to the same pool of knowledge. As Postman puts it: "Children are a group of people who do *not* know certain things that adults know. In the Middle Ages there were no children because there existed no means for adults to know exclusive information. In the Age of Gutenberg, such a means developed."[5] In this sense, then, adults and children were equally childish.

There were other factors that promoted the development of the separate sphere of childhood. One was the notion of privacy, which evolved gradually over the centuries. Until the 18th century, the average person spent almost no time alone. Sleeping was communal, and through the 16th and 17th centuries even the middle class lived in large extended-family homes. Only with the idea that certain rooms and spaces could be designated as off-limits could the possibility of shielding children from certain kinds of behavior take hold. It wasn't until the 17th century that rooms with designated functions began to appear — most notably, bedrooms, which made privacy for sex possible for the first time.

The other important factor was the spread of universal compulsory education. In the Middle Ages, once they grew beyond infancy, most children worked as manual laborers. Only the children of the nobility and those adopted as oblates by monasteries and religious orders received anything resembling a formal education. Beginning in the early 19th century, partly in response to concerns about the exploitation of child factory workers, even some of the children of the working class began to attend school. For the first time, there was a whole group of people who were off doing something else, separated from the rest of the population for a large part of the day. Removed from the daily activities of society, schoolchildren were considered a breed apart. The introduction of universal education thus created a new schism between adult and child.

This creation of the separate sphere of childhood also ushered in a new philosophy of protectiveness; the idea that children have special needs that are different from those of adults and that require them to be treated differently. This philosophic strain has given rise to, among other things, the modern institution of child welfare agencies and various child-protection laws. An obvious example of the latter is the movement to outlaw child labor. In the Middle Ages, children performed various kinds of work — domestic chores, working the fields, apprenticing — as they typically do in all agrarian, non-industrial societies. But the triumph of industrialism radically changed the nature of child labor. The children of impoverished families — many as young as five and six years old — were forced to toil for long hours in the mines and factories — the "dark Satanic mills" of the industrial revolution. A series of acts were passed in 19th century Britain that imposed restrictions on employers' use of child workers, establishing age requirements and limits to the number of hours they were allowed to work. Similar legal restrictions were adopted in North America and throughout Europe, though it wasn't until nearly the end of the century that the practice was finally outlawed altogether. (Of course, like child abandonment, child labor persists in many parts of the world today, a fact that has spawned a renewed global movement against the practice, spearheaded by groups such as Canada's Save the Children, which I'll discuss in a later chapter.)

In some cases, the differential treatment of children was legally mandated, as it was in the child labor laws. In other areas, the gradual evolution of different social customs was more important. For instance, certain kinds of sexually charged interactions between adults and children were common in the Middle Ages, as we know from accounts of servants "teasing" babies by playing with their genitals. But once sexual activity was removed from children's purview, more definite boundaries began to be laid down around what constituted acceptable touching of children by adults. Over the subsequent centuries, the idea took hold that children should to be afforded some measure of protection from sexual abuse, and acts that were once casually tolerated are now not only considered socially taboo, but are legally outlawed as well.

These days, we accept as a given that there are numerous situations in which children need to be treated differently from adults. The need for age restrictions on certain activities is one example. But even there, the rules aren't hard and fast, and changes in technology keep getting ahead of existing regulations. Until laws were brought in mandating the minimum driving age in North America, children under sixteen routinely drove cars, especially in rural areas. Similarly, when those scourges of the waterways known as Personal Watercraft (PWC) first came on the market here in the eighties, there were no age restrictions on who could operate them. In Ontario, a rash of incidents in recent years — including the deaths of two joyriding fourteen-year-olds, and a nine-year-old girl who suffered severe head injuries when the PWC she was driving crashed into a boat — has put pressure on the provincial government to legislate age restrictions for PWCs.

There's no doubt that the development of the separate protected sphere of childhood has been one of the great historical advances of modern times, and that it has made the lives of children materially better. But protectiveness can be a double-edged sword, because it's always accompanied by some degree of hierarchy and power imbalance. Traditionally, women have also been considered weak and in need of protection — a status that has gone hand-in-hand with their powerlessness in society. Relative to the adults in their lives, children are in a position of powerlessness that has distinct similarities to the way women were viewed until well into the 20th century in Western society. Challenges to the fundamental power imbalance between children and adults have arisen periodically throughout history, most forcefully during the turbulent decade of the seventies when, along with all the other liberation movements, the idea that children had rights began to be seriously discussed.

Kids' Lib

In North America, the various political movements of the sixties and seventies — Civil Rights activism, the struggle against the Vietnam War, Women's Liberation — ushered in a radical re-thinking of many time-honored institutions, including the family and the education system. In this climate of debate and social upheaval, a number of activists began to apply the rhetoric of liberation to young people, and put forward the notion that, like women and black people, children were an oppressed group that needed to challenge the prevailing power structure. Writers R.D. Laing and David Cooper published harsh critiques of traditional psychological theory, particularly as it pertained to child rearing and the family. These radical therapists proposed that the nuclear family itself was the problem, as parents were the source of much of children's oppression.

Another advocate of this view was historian Lloyd de Mause. In his 1974 book, *The History of Childhood,* de Mause examines childhood in Western history through a psychoanalytic lens, a particular approach for which he invented the term "psychohistory." The book's dramatic opening statement that "the history of childhood is a nightmare from which we have only recently begun to awaken" leaves no doubt about de Mause's strong point of view. In his scheme, most parents through the centuries have been unable to feel true empathy for their children, because they're in the grip of fear and resentment of children's natural vitality. Consequently, adults exhibit a deep-seated need to control and "civilize" children, to keep them in their place. In de Mause's view, the bulk of human history has been marked by adults' naked abuse of their power over children, and his exhaustive catalogue of harmful and punitive child-rearing practices — the swaddling of infants to keep them passive and quiet, the use of leading-strings and other devices to prevent babies from "animal-like" crawling, not to mention beating, abandonment and infanticide — has a persuasive power. But overall, his argument is weakened by the use of sweeping generalizations and an approach to history colored by a psychological bias that judges the past by the standards of the present.

A different, but equally passionate, line of thinking was offered by the influential education critic John Holt. His book, *Escape from Childhood: The Needs and Rights of Children,* published the same year as de Mause's, argues that modern childhood is a kind of prison, a "walled garden" of powerlessness and enforced ignorance that denies children their basic rights as human beings. Holt calls for an "escape from childhood" — in essence, the complete elimination of the separate sphere that has taken hold in Western culture since the Middle Ages — and advocates granting children the full range of rights and privileges that adults enjoy.

Though he argues for a profound change in the power relations between adults and children, Holt doesn't completely dismiss the notion that adults should have authority over children. But he does make a crucial distinction between different kinds of authority. In Holt's view, children's respect for their elders should stem from what he calls the natural authority arising from adults' "greater skill, knowledge, experience, courage, commitment or concern," as opposed to "authority which rests only on force, the power to threaten, punish and hurt."[6] Children, Holt argues, readily perceive the difference between the two, and respond positively to natural authority.

Many of Holt's prescriptions are impractical and, on the face of it, some border on the preposterous. He's in favor of allowing children of any age the right to vote in elections, hold down jobs and live wherever they choose, among other things. But I think it's a mistake to dismiss *Escape from Childhood* as some quaint artifact of seventies' liberation rhetoric, as Neil Postman has done. Many of the things Holt calls for are coming to pass, though not necessarily in the way he envisioned. Children as young as eleven and twelve hold down "jobs" on the Internet and choose to live on the streets rather than at home. And there's no doubt that, since the notion of children's liberation was first raised in the seventies, many young people have come to expect they'll be listened to and taken seriously. At the core of Holt's thesis is a deep respect for children, a belief in their abilities, and an attempt to conjure up a vision of what a truly equal relationship between adults and children might look like. *Escape from Childhood* offers a bracing re-examination of some of our most deeply entrenched beliefs about children, the full implications of which have yet to be dealt with.

Not In Front Of The Children!

In many ways, Holt's "escape from childhood" has already occurred, but through cultural expression, not the political change he predicted. During the sixties and seventies, Marshall McLuhan created a stir with his theories on how advances in communications technology were bringing about radical changes in society. Everyone had televisions, of course, but the idea that television was changing our way of life — even the very way we think about and experience the world, as McLuhan argued — was still new and provocative. By the time Neil Postman wrote *The Disappearance of Childhood* in the early eighties, he could unilaterally state that childhood was dead, and that television had killed it, a theme he picks up again in his most recent book, *Building a Bridge to the Eighteenth Century*:

> If the technology of a culture makes it impossible to conceal anything from the young, in what sense can we say childhood exists? Yes, as always, we have young, small people among us. But if, by seven or eight or even eleven and twelve, they have access to the same infor-

mation as do adults, how do adults guide their future? What does a forty-year-old have to teach a twelve-year-old if both of them have been seeing the same TV programs, the same movies, the same new shows, listening to the same CDs and calling forth the same information on the Internet? [7]

Postman believes that literacy and book learning "represented an almost unqualified triumph over our animal nature." He also proposes that a sense of shame regarding our bodily functions — the animal parts of ourselves — is an essential element in the process of becoming civilized. In his view, these two things lie at the very root of childhood: a well-developed sense of shame, and the keeping of secrets. Therefore maintaining the separate realm of childhood is crucial to our collective well-being. Postman concludes that the rise of mass media, and television in particular, is responsible for the inexorable erosion of the separate, protected realm of childhood that was first created by the rise of literacy. This constitutes, in his view, an unmitigated social disaster in human history, a spiraling descent into a latter-day Dark Ages of illiteracy and irrationality. *Building a Bridge* is a brilliantly argued polemic that expresses a deeply pessimistic (and, in my view, wrong-headed) view of the future of childhood.

The same analytical framework informs the work of another important commentator on modern childhood, sociologist Joshua Meyerowitz. But his approach is analytical rather than polemical: in his book, *No Sense of Place: The Impact of Electronic Media on Social Behavior,* Meyerowitz explores some of the specifics of how mass media are transforming the experience of childhood. Like Postman, he also points to literacy as the single most important factor in creating the separate realm of childhood. "Literacy created childhood and adulthood," he states succinctly. The development of print allowed for an "adult conspiracy" in which children were not even supposed to be aware that important knowledge was being kept hidden from them. This is what Meyerowitz calls the secret of secrecy:

What is revolutionary about television is not that it necessarily gives children 'adult minds', but that it allows the very young child to be 'present' at adult interactions. Television removes barriers that once divided people of different ages and reading abilities ... Young children may not fully understand the issues of sex, death, crime and money that are presented to them on television. Or, put differently, they may understand these issues only in childlike ways. Yet television nevertheless exposes them to many topics and behaviors that adults have spent several centuries trying to keep hidden from children." [8]

Besides sex and death, perhaps the one "cultural secret" that adults have the greatest investment in maintaining is the illusion of their own perfection, and that, too, is revealed to children by television. By showing the imperfections of adults to children, TV effectively undermines the authority of grown-ups. It does this by raising the curtain on what Meyerowitz calls the backstage of adult life, exposing the insecurities, the pettiness and the simple ineffectualness that parents are normally loathe to let children witness. In essence, TV lays bare all those things that used to make grown-ups exclaim: "Not in front of the children!"

Meyerowitz presents a fascinating analysis of an episode of the popular mid-fifties series *Father Knows Best,* in which the parents, Jim and Margaret, are angry at one another but try to keep their children from finding out. When the kids inadvertently witness an argument, they are so convinced that their parents never fight that they decide that Jim and Margaret must just be kidding around. As Meyerowitz points out, while the child-characters in the show may be sheltered from knowing the truth, the children *watching* the program have a whole different perspective, seeing "both the hidden behavior and the process of sheltering it from children." So sitcoms and family dramas, by portraying these kinds of scenes of domestic life, reveal Meyerowitz's "secret of secrecy" to young viewers time and time again. What has changed in present-day shows like *The Simpsons* (and what distresses so many adults) is that even the pretense of parental competence has been cast aside. Jim and Margaret may have felt the need to conceal their imperfections from the kids in *Father Knows Best,* but Homer Simpson's burping, befuddled, bumbling ways are sprawled out on the couch for the whole family — on both sides of the TV screen — to see.

Innocence vs. Ignorance

Ask a person why it's so important to shield children from things like sex and death and the reply is almost invariably that these things have to be kept from children in order to preserve their innocence. This is one of the most deeply held notions in our culture. But what is the nature of this childhood innocence we try to protect so tenaciously? Are children truly innocent? In what way?

The notion of childhood innocence saw its beginnings in the Romantic period, and found particular expression in the writings of Jean-Jacques Rousseau. The Romantics seized on the child as a symbol of all the things they exalted — the beauty of nature, the primacy of instinct — and their view has colored our thinking about childhood right to the present day. Rousseau's seminal book, *Emile,* first published in 1762, explored the idea of a young child growing up in a state of nature, uncorrupted by civilization. Rousseau's revolutionary thesis was that the child was important as a person, not just as a work-in-progress or a miniature adult, and that the natural impulses of children were deeply, inherently good. He took issue with John Locke, who considered the young child as a clean slate, something for adults to shape, mold and fill with knowledge. However, for all that he advocated lavishing attention on a single child in *Emile,* Rousseau was not interested in raising his own children and abandoned them to orphanages. In current parlance, he talked the talk but didn't walk the walk. Nevertheless, his ideas on children and childhood have been enormously influential.

The poetry of William Blake, which makes abundant use of the imagery of childhood, also sprang from the Romantic tradition. Blake's *Songs of Innocence* were explorations of what he saw as the young child's state of grace, a purity of soul that inevitably, in his *Songs of Experience*, had to encounter the pain of existence. Blake was one of the first adults to adopt, without irony or embarrassment, the voice and perspective of the young child: "I have no name: I am but two days old," he writes in "Infant Joy." In "The Echoing Green," another poem from *Songs of Innocence*, the garden is identified with nature and freedom from care. But Blake's view of childhood was subsequently sentimentalized and taken to extremes — particularly by the Victorians — in the cherubic figures of children by artists such as Kate Greenaway and Arthur Rackham. It was these Victorian artists as well as children's writers like Beatrix Potter who also brought to full flower (no pun intended) the garden metaphor that has become so identified with our ideas about childhood.

The idea of the freedom to play was also at the root of German educator Friedrich Froebel's innovation of *kindergarten* — literally translated as "children's garden." But this innovation was also a classroom, a space set apart for young children, and so the modern kindergarten suggests at its very root the separation of children from the adult world. John Holt aptly drew on this aspect of the metaphor when he described modern childhood as a "walled garden" in *Escape from Childhood*. In doing so he illuminated the flip side of the metaphor, for a walled garden may be a beautiful place, but the children in it are certainly not free to come and go as they please. And to a large extent, the "beauty" of the garden rests on the absence of those things the wall is designed to keep out.

Therein lies the conundrum of our culture's view of childhood: it is based on *not-knowing*. The primary meaning of the word innocent is "free from moral wrong, sinless" — a state of inherent goodness that certainly seems to match what most of us believe about children. It's the secondary (and likely older) meaning of "innocent" that has to do with ignorance, with naïveté, with the state of being unacquainted with pain and evil and unpleasantness. Which brings us back to Postman's statement that "without secrets there can be no childhood." So many of our beliefs about children's innocence are tied up the necessity of keeping them in the dark about sexuality and the harsher aspects of life.

The Medveds certainly share this view in *Saving Childhood.* Though their entire book is predicated on the need to preserve childhood innocence, they never define clearly what they mean. They seem to believe that it's one of those universally shared assumptions — something you can't put your finger on, but that you know when you see it. The entire concluding section of *Saving Childhood* gives the Medveds' prescription for how to preserve and reinforce innocence: by promoting a sense of security, a sense of wonder for the world and optimism for the future. Certainly not a list that too many people would quarrel with — it's precisely the kind of legacy that any society would want to pass on to its young. And yet all the causes of this loss of innocence, in their view, have to do with kids' increased knowledge of the world. The childhood innocence we hold so dear seems to have less to do with children's inherent goodness than it does with their enforced ignorance of certain wide swaths of human behavior. Childhood innocence depends, then, on a lack, an absence. Seen from this vantage point, it's a negative rather than a positive state of being.

But can we be so sure that innocence depends on ignorance? Maybe they're two entirely separate things. Maybe children can gain knowledge of the adult world without losing their innocence.

I want to try to shed a bit more light on this question by discussing the work of anthropologist Ashley Montagu. In his book, *Growing Young,* he proposes what appears superficially to be a view of childhood similar to the Medveds', but with some important differences. *Growing Young,* first published in the early eighties, is an exploration of the human aging process and of what becomes of those qualities we most associate with childhood, such as simplicity, curiosity, openness to new ideas, joyfulness and emotional directness. Montagu examines how our notion of maturity is largely viewed as a casting-off of these qualities, and how this belief is conveyed to children: "(The child) comes to identify 'growing up' in height with 'growing up' in adult stature. The conventional wisdom requires that all 'childish' traits be left behind just as one does one's outworn clothes."[9]

In *Growing Young* he makes the radical suggestion that humans have got this maturity business all wrong, that we shouldn't try to grow up, but to grow young, to hang on to these childlike qualities as we age. Though Montagu's list of desirable traits is much the same (though even more comprehensive) than the Medveds', I think it's significant that he largely avoids using the word innocence in his discussion. In fact, nowhere in his book does Montagu propose that ignorance of sexuality and other adult matters is a necessary or positive aspect of childhood. Instead, he focuses on children's curiosity, their powerful need to know, to find out and to discover, and on what he calls their innate compassionate intelligence. I think Montagu's perspective on childhood in *Growing Young* gives us a basis for understanding the notion — as difficult as it may be for us to get our heads around — that children can be innocent without being kept ignorant. That it's not being kept in the dark about sex and death that keeps children so open, sensitive and optimistic. Conversely, that their awareness of these things isn't going to "rob them of their childhood" and do damage to those qualities we rightly value.

At this point in our history, we're in a state of enormous flux. Many of our old certainties no longer apply. Yet no matter how starkly the walled garden of childhood may be crumbling, many of us obstinately persist in our efforts to shore it up. Nowhere is this more obvious — and our efforts more clearly in vain — than in the Unholy Trinity of sex, death and swearing.

NOTES

1. Neil Postman, *Building a Bridge to the Eighteenth Century: How the Past Can Improve Our Future* (New York: Alfred A. Knopf, 1999), 116.
2. Philippe Ariès, *Centuries of Childhood,* translated from the French by Robert Baldick (New York: Vintage Books, 1962), 61.
3. Ibid., 128.
4. Ibid., 38-39.
5. Neil Postman, *The Disappearance of Childhood* (New York: Delacorte, 1982), 85.
6. John Holt, *Escape From Childhood: The Needs and Rights of Children* (New York: E.P. Dutton, 1974), 200-201.
7. Postman, *Building a Bridge to the Eighteenth Century,* 125.
8. Joshua Meyerowitz, *No Sense of Place: The Impact of Electronic Media on Social Behavior* (New York: Oxford University Press, 1985), 246-247.
9. Ashley Montagu, *Growing Young* (New York: McGraw-Hill, 1981), 196.

THE UNHOLY TRINITY

Please understand that this movie was a very vulgar movie — and we tell you how vulgar it is. I will soon forget this movie — no problem — I just wish I could forget the sight of the eight- or nine-year-old little girl in the audience ... with her parents.

Ulp. That could have been me and Ivy.

The reviewer quoted above was writing from Dallas, Texas, the home base of CAPalert, a Christian Website that serves as a moral watchdog of pop culture. And Ivy was more like ten or eleven when she talked me into taking her to one of Toronto's gigantic multiplexes to see *Austin Powers: The Spy Who Shagged Me.* Like CAPalert's correspondent, we were bummed out by the movie. My main problem wasn't that it was vulgar (though I must say I could've done without the sight of Fat Bastard imbibing the liquid stool sample), but that it was so completely unfunny. Ivy, more forgiving as kids usually are, declared it a dud overall, but thought it had a few funny moments.

Back in the fifties and sixties, when I was growing up, there were movies for kids and movies for grown-ups, and parents had no trouble figuring out which was which. Kids could see movies made expressly for them, like Disney's *Bambi* and *101 Dalmatians,* as well as "family" films and musicals like *Oklahoma* and *The Sound of Music.*

Everything else — westerns, dramas, foreign films — was pretty much off-limits. The lines were clearly drawn. Deciding whether or not to take the kids to see a given movie was — as they say — strictly a no-brainer.

Talk about changing times. In the summer of 1999, for example, *Austin Powers* was vying with *Big Daddy* for the top spot at the box office, as teenagers and pre-teens flocked to these raunchy Mike Myers and Adam Sandler comedies. But even six- and seven-year-olds were begging their parents to take them to *Big Daddy* and *Austin Powers*. It isn't all that surprising: *Big Daddy* features a cute five-year-old who gets adopted by Sandler's character, and *Austin Powers* has Myers' grossly bad teeth plus an adorable midget named Mini-Me. But the sight of Myers "shagging" various babes, or Sandler tripping up unsuspecting rollerbladers and demonstrating how to urinate in public places left a lot of horrified parents wishing they'd stuck to their guns and trundled the little ones off to see Disney's *Tarzan* instead.

So just what is a "kids' movie" these days? Good luck trying to figure that one out.

Not only has the distinction between adult's and children's films become hopelessly blurred, but the way we watch movies has changed. Many kids nowadays see a lot more movies on home video than in movie theatres, and there's no way parents can keep up with all the new releases. Often, adults haven't got a clue what's in the movies that kids are asking them to rent. This was brought home to me when parents began approaching me in the video store to ask whether *There's Something About Mary* was suitable. "Ah, do you know about the hair gel scene?" I'd ask, usually to be met with a blank stare. I attempted — in the most delicate way possible — to describe the scene in which Cameron Diaz's character smears a certain male bodily fluid on her hair, mistaking it for styling gel. But *Mary*, at least, was a fairly sweet-natured comedy at heart. I was a bit taken aback when, not long ago, Ivy announced to me that she'd seen the movie *Election* on video at a friend's birthday party. Now, I'm a great admirer of this darkly satirical film, but even I have to admit that it's pretty raw stuff for a bunch of eleven-year-olds at a sleepover. Sure enough, it turned out that the parent of the girl hosting the party had no idea what the movie was about. The girls wanted to see it because it starred Reese Witherspoon, and this mother assumed it was another generic teen comedy.

But wait a minute. Isn't this the very problem the movie ratings system was designed to take care of? *Yeah, right,* you can almost hear the kids snickering. *As if anybody takes them seriously!* Even when parents do bother to check a movie's rating beforehand (in my experience, parents rely far more on word-of-mouth than on ratings) it doesn't necessarily give them any meaningful information about what kids are going to see. *Big Daddy* and *Austin Powers,* for example, were both rated PG-13.*

But I think it's likely that both movies would have received an R rating even a few years earlier. As a demonstration of just how arbitrary the ratings system can be, consider the case of *Billy Elliot,* a critically acclaimed British film that was released late in 2000. The story concerns an eleven-year-old boy who struggles against the macho culture of his coal-mining town to realize his dream of becoming a ballet dancer. Despite the fact that the film is a feel-good, inspirational story with no sex or violence, *Billy Elliot* was given an R rating by the MPAA solely on the basis of the forty-odd profanities that pepper the dialogue.

Perhaps nothing exposed the growing irrelevancy of the ratings system and how little bearing it has on what kids get to see as the controversy on the eve of the American Presidential election in 2000,

---

*For the sake of clarity and convenience, I use the Motion Picture Association of America (MPAA) ratings throughout most of this book. Ontario and other Canadian provinces have their own separate ratings systems, which don't correspond exactly to those of the MPAA. In Ontario, for example, the nearest counterpart to PG-13 is 14A, a new rating adopted in 2001. But while the MPAA warns only that films in the PG13 category may not be suitable for those under thirteen, the Ontario Film Review Board requires children under fourteen to be accompanied by an adult.

when a U.S. Federal Trade Commission report revealed that Hollywood was target-marketing R-rated movies to children under seventeen. The report documented that kids as young as nine had participated in studio-sponsored focus groups, where they were shown R-rated films like *I Still Know What You Did Last Summer* and *The Fifth Element*. Critics like Senator John McCain launched scathing attacks on the big studios, accusing them of hypocrisy in ignoring their own ratings systems. But Hollywood was only acting on what everyone already knew: kids *do* see R-rated movies. In fact, as far as many teenagers are concerned, PG-13 movies are for the little squirts. "Any movie worth going to," one told an Associated Press reporter, "is R-rated."

The current confusion is also responsible for the growing popularity of parents' guides to new movies and video releases. These guides used to be confined to parenting magazines, but increasingly they're turning up everywhere — in daily newspapers, in mainstream magazines, on Internet sites — and many parents have come to rely on them to decide which movies kids should be allowed to see. One thing that's struck me as I've surveyed these guides is that they're not particularly concerned with the *quality* of the movies, which, when you really think about it, is a bit curious. After all, when critics review a movie for adults, they're concerned with artistic questions, such as: What's the movie's theme? What distinguishes it stylistically from other films? Is it worth seeing? Why or why not? But these kinds of considerations carry little or no weight in this case. In some ways, this just reflects the widespread belief that children's entertainment is largely outside the realm of art (or worse, that kids have no taste, so that if they like something, it must be *bad* art). There are exceptions, of course. Some of these guides, like *Entertainment Weekly's*, actually ask the question "Will Kids Want to Watch it?" But for the most part, parents' guides aren't concerned with questions of quality, because the people consulting them aren't particularly interested in whether a movie's good or bad. What they really want to know is whether there's any sex, violence or bad language in it. Informing parents about this Unholy Trinity has become pretty much the whole raison d'être of these guides, as it is of the ratings systems themselves.

How did sex, violence and profanity come to be at the very core of our anxieties about childhood? The belief that we have to keep these things away from kids' eyes and ears is deeply rooted. Even the baby boomers who were part of the sexual revolution, used cusswords freely and "let it all hang out" in the sixties and seventies are now among those parents who adamantly insist on shielding children. But maybe it's time to ask ourselves: Just what is it we're so afraid of? What's so dangerous about sex, violence and profanity? The average North American twelve-year-old has already had several years of sexual education in school, and heard every swear word in existence on the latest Eminem CD.

So what's the big deal? Why do we fight so hard to shield kids from things they already know?

Falling Taboos

Someone, somewhere must have actually made good on the warning, "I'll wash your mouth out with soap!" But in truth, it's one of those pat phrases, an empty threat many parents used to make when they caught kids swearing. You don't hear it much anymore, but that doesn't mean parents have gotten blasé about what comes out of kids' mouths. In fact, Rick Bray, an Arkansas computer programmer, got so upset, he set out to root the problem out at the source. Bray is the inventor of TV Guardian, a device that bleeps out offensive words in TV programs and videos by reading the encoded closed-captioning text used for hearing-impaired viewers and substituting alternative, milder phrases. Thus "don't fuck with me" is rendered by TV Guardian as "don't wow with me," and "Beavis and Butthead" becomes, believe it or not, "Beavis and Jerk." In effect, with TV Guardian, Bray's found a way to wash the TV's mouth out with soap.

Mind you, the kids watching still know exactly what's being said (and probably find the whole exercise hilarious — far more entertaining than regular TV). But TV Guardian and a similar device called Curse-Free TV make the parents who buy them feel like they're fighting the good fight against declining language standards.

Examples of what you might call the TV Guardian mindset are everywhere in children's entertainment. I saw this first-hand a couple of years ago when I attended an international children's film festival in Toronto to review movies for my radio column. I took along Ivy, then ten, as guest critic. Festivals aimed at children, especially ones that showcase foreign-language films with English subtitles, are still relative rarities. A distinct departure from the more typical Disney-style children's entertainment, festivals such as Toronto's Sprockets and the International Children's Film Festival in Chicago attract a more sophisticated audience of children and adults than the typical multiplex.

At Sprockets, Ivy and I were particularly taken with a warmly funny Scandinavian film called *The Master Detective and Rasmus*, based on a series of popular Swedish mystery-adventure stories. One of the things I liked about the film was its refreshingly realistic portrayal of kids. Though at times they did foolish things and were nasty to one another, they weren't particularly dysfunctional. And though they were mostly cheerful, resourceful, and basically honest, they were miles away from the pseudo-wholesome, self-conscious cuteness that plagues so many of Hollywood's portrayals of kids.

For the benefit of children too young to read, the festival organizers thoughtfully provided someone at each screening to read the subtitles out loud. Early on in the film, small-town kids who are members of rival secret societies stage a mock battle. As the losers run away, the three victors call laughingly after them: "That's right, run, you little shits!" But when the festival's reader got to this bit of dialogue, she substituted it with "you little rats" or something like that. This, despite the fact that "you little shits" was written plain as day, right up there on the screen.

Several more of these word-substitutions occurred in the course of the film. I didn't know if it was the reader's instinctive choice or the festival's cautious policy. Surely, I thought, bowdlerizing a mild, everyday profanity like shit isn't necessary for a sophisticated, urban audience like this. Yet when the movie was over, I overheard a mother and daughter talking about the film. "Wasn't that good?" the girl said eagerly. But the mother clearly didn't share her daughter's enthusiasm, and I found her reply — "Some of the language certainly wasn't very good!" — disheartening. Here was a charming children's film with real artistic integrity, and the first thing out of this mother's mouth was the typical adult knee-jerk complaint about bad language.

It would be difficult to overstate just how enormous a shift has taken place around language taboos in the past few decades. Swear words used to be for men only, used only in the presence of other men, and never in public. Now women swear as much as men — at least in some social circles — and kids hear profanity in movies, on CDs, and right on their own streets. "Damn," "hell" and even "bitch," which were never uttered in public when I was a kid, are now commonplace. A yawning gap has developed between the generations; modern kids have a much more casual attitude toward profanity than their elders. One baffled teacher told a reporter for the *Wall Street Journal* that her students "haven't even got a concept of obscenity." And it's true. When they hear a word like fuck, kids today just don't have the same adrenaline rush of shock mingled with shame as people who grew up in the era when such words were strictly forbidden.

Traditionally, profanity has been used to express extreme emotions — rage, excitement, disgust — that are, in a sense, *beyond* words; too primitive for normal, everyday speech. In fact, that's precisely the problem with one of the most typical responses to profanity: "Can't they find a more intelligent way to express themselves?" No, they can't, because where this kind of raw, undiluted emotion is concerned, intelligence is pretty much beside the point. Despite the profound social shift in attitudes, swear words still carry a powerful charge. Research into the neurological condition Tourette's Syndrome, for which involuntary cursing is a frequent symptom, shows that these words spring from a different, more primitive part of the brain than everyday speech. Do we lose something in diluting this powerful cultural taboo, as we progressively become more tolerant, even blasé, about profanity? We're in uncharted territory here, and no one really knows the answer.

What we do know is that language taboos vary from culture to culture, and that some, perhaps most, other societies have considerably more relaxed standards of what's permissible to talk about in the presence of children. It's also likely that adults in medieval Europe swore freely within earshot of children, probably using many of the same words we do today. ("Fuck" is known to have been in use for more than 500 years.) It could be argued that the normalization of swearing is one of the ways in which we're reverting to medieval norms of behavior, an idea I'll develop further in the next chapter.

Though few people will openly admit to being comfortable with the general loosening of language taboos, we're all trying to feel our way through this new reality. Parents still dutifully go through the motions of chastising kids, telling them, "We don't use language like that in this house." But the truth is, many of us *do*. In the privacy of our homes, within our own social circles, a lot of us draw casually on the vocabulary of traditional profanities and barely even notice ourselves doing it. In my own household, "shit" and "goddamn" are no-big-deal daily occurrences. Words like "fuck" and "asshole" make less frequent appearances, and an even stronger term like "motherfucker" would be reserved, so to speak, for special occasions. But even in our house, there are still limits and taboos. I doubt that either of my children has ever heard me say the word "cunt." It's a word I rarely use, because I'm unable to say or hear it without flinching. (I even feel uncomfortable as I type it.) It makes no rational sense to even make that kind of distinction. But then, there's something about our response to the truly profane that is deeply, fundamentally irrational — which is probably as it should be.

We never sat down and worked out a family policy on swearing. It just evolved. Our kids grew up hearing certain words in certain situations, and figured out that they were just as free to use them in our presence as we were in theirs. (My observation, though, is that kids aren't really comfortable using words stronger than "shit" and don't — unless they're actively seeking to shock the adults around them — until they're well into their teens.) We warned our daughters from the time they were very young that attitudes were different in the outside world, especially in places like school and among people from older generations, many of whom didn't share our views. We encouraged them to be prudent, to avoid swearing in situations where it would offend someone (unless, of course, they *wanted* to offend someone). To our knowledge, they pretty much followed this advice without difficulty.

Sex, Kids and Videotape

One of the more bizarre developments of the nineties (even more bizarre than TV Guardian) was the periodic waves of controversy swirling around Disney films. Since the beginning of the decade, almost every animated feature released by Disney has been the subject of media stories, Internet rumours and urban legends claiming that there's hidden sexual content in the films. It all began with the supposed image of an erect penis in *The Little Mermaid*, followed by claims a few years later that the word "sex" was spelled out in a dust cloud in *The Lion King*. When Aladdin came out on video in 1994, some parents claimed they could hear *Aladdin* muttering the words "good teenagers, take off your clothes" under his breath. These incidents reached a nadir of sorts in early 1999 with the video release of a 1977 film, *The Rescuers,* which was found to contain a brief image of a woman's naked breasts. Despite the fact that the offending image appeared only in two frames of the film and wasn't detectable in normal viewing, Disney responded swiftly to the controversy by recalling over 3 million video copies of *The Rescuers.*

As each one of these stories broke, there was much media speculation, peppered with frame-by-frame examinations of the offending videos: Did that cloud over Simba's head really spell out S-E-X? Just what was Aladdin mumbling to that tiger? (Personally, I couldn't make head or tail of it.) There's a longstanding tradition in animation of artists inserting hard-to-detect private jokes, a practice that certainly isn't unknown at a studio the size of Disney. But whether the images were really there, or were simply the products of overzealous parental imaginations, is beside the point. What's fascinating about these incidents is the intensity of the reaction they engendered, both on the part of the company and the super-vigilant parents.

The objectionable images and dialogue, if they were really there, were pretty tame — nothing kids today can't see in a typical lingerie ad. But the idea that anything remotely sexual might crop up, however fleetingly, in a Disney movie was too much at odds with its carefully cultivated, family-values image. *The Rescuers* incident was the first time the company had ever issued a mass product recall, and despite the cost, the company clearly felt it was worth it. As a spokesperson put it at the time: "We want parents to know they can rely on the Disney brand."

Perhaps the only way to make sense of these brouhahas is to view them as a form of mass hysteria, springing from a desperate need to over-compensate. These days, our kids are living in a virtual sea of sexual imagery — on prime-time TV, and especially in advertising — a fact we're profoundly uncomfortable with, but feel powerless to do anything about. So we patrol even more vigorously those parts of our children's lives we *can* have some influence on. We turn to Disney as an oasis of old-fashioned, squeaky-clean values, and our outrage is all the greater when we suspect the company isn't keeping up its end of the bargain. For if parents can't rely on the inheritors of Uncle Walt's legacy to shore up the walled garden of childhood, just who can they trust to do it?

Not that there aren't some perfectly good reasons for keeping aspects of sexuality hidden from children. It's a grown-up activity meant to be done with at least a modicum of privacy. And as boundless as kids' curiosity can be, sex is one of those things they don't really *want* to know a lot about. Of course, children do experience sexual sensations; they get pleasure from touching themselves and one another. But sweaty, grinding sex, as adults do it, is simply not an activity children naturally want to engage in (despite the self-justifying arguments of child molesters). It may well be that the best reason for keeping sex out of children's entertainment isn't because it will corrupt them, but simply because it doesn't *belong*. Once robbed of that "forbidden fruit" allure, sex is not something they're all that interested in.

Still, confusion swirls around this issue, as parents are more and more concerned about what's acceptable and what's not. For the past several decades, games like "doctor" and "you show me yours and I'll show you mine" have been looked upon as part of kids' normal exploratory play. But recently, with our heightened awareness of sexual abuse, there are worries about when these activities might cross the line that separates harmless play from exploitation. This question was at the crux of a controversial 1999 case in which an eleven-year-old Swiss–American boy was arrested in Colorado after a neighbor spied him "inappropriately touching" his younger sister. The charges against the boy were eventually dropped and he returned with his family to Switzerland.

Colorado was also the site of an earlier, even more notorious case that brought the issue of children and sexuality to the fore. JonBenet Ramsey, murdered by an (at this writing) unknown assailant in 1997, had been a frequent participant in child beauty pageants. After her death, the media fed on ubiquitous photos and video clips of the heavily made-up six-year-old decked out in provocative outfits. The Ramsey case fueled growing concerns that childhood itself is becoming more sexualized, that kids are dressing suggestively, and showing an interest in sex at earlier ages than ever before. This issue became

a media preoccupation in the late nineties with the Spice Girls phenomenon. Parents were horrified to see their little girls, many as
young as five and six, dressing in skimpy halter tops, striking come-
hither poses and lip-synching "Come a little closer, baby, get it on,
get it on, 'cause tonight is the night when two become one."
Newspapers and magazines trumpeted headlines like, "Is Spicemania
turning little girls into sex kittens?"

But fears about the sexualization of childhood go back a lot further than the Spice Girls. In fact, if anyone's responsible for putting
sex in modern childhood, it's Ruth Handler, the creator of Barbie.
When Handler first developed the doll for Mattel back in the fifties,
Barbie was a radical departure from previous dolls, which were
invariably baby-dolls meant to be "mothered" by their little-girl
owners. Handler first got the idea for a grown-up doll from watching young girls playing with paper dolls, endlessly changing their
cut-out outfits. When she heard about a German doll named Lilli
and saw Lilli's mature, elongated body and fully developed breasts,
Handler knew she'd found the model for her new doll, which she
named Barbie after her own daughter. Her fellow (and mostly male)
executives at Mattel objected; they told Handler it looked too sexy,
that mothers would never buy it for their little girls. But Handler
was convinced that North America was ready for a grown-up doll as
long as its sexiness was of the squeaky-clean variety (which is still as
good a description of Barbie as any). Her instincts, of course, were
proven right: although parents were initially wary of the curvaceous
new toy, Barbie was an immediate hit with girls, who wore down
their parents' resistance — just as they've done more recently with
the Spice Girls.

Part of the problem of "sexualized" childhood lies in our own
perceptions of it. Seven-year-old girls may dress up like the Spice
Girls and mimic their routines, but that doesn't mean they want to
be sexual. When we call their behavior sexy or provocative, that's our
adult projection. To the kids themselves, it's dress-up, fantasy for

their own amusement. For children, sexuality is like a lot of other aspects of adult life — something they want to play with and try on for size. Though they may seem superficially similar, there's actually a world of difference between this kind of dress-up and the child beauty pageants JonBenet Ramsey participated in. There, young contestants compete for cash prizes and perform for the amusement of adults. The parents insist, as JonBenet's mother did, that the kids want to participate, that the pageants are innocent fun. But the thinly veiled sexuality of the whole exercise is inescapable. In many ways, child beauty pageants are just an updated version of the old Shirley Temple movies, in which no one — on-screen or off — appeared to notice that there was anything the least bit odd or inappropriate about having a six-year-old dressed up as a chorus girl in lacy black lingerie.

Do child beauty pageants and the trend toward ever-younger fashion models encourage sexual abuse, by making it more socially acceptable to view children as sex objects? It's a fair question, one that shouldn't be dismissed out of hand. But it's worth keeping in mind that the sexual abuse of children has been going on for centuries. Whether it's more widespread today than in the past is impossible to determine; we simply don't have the evidence one way or another. The steady stream of long-hidden anecdotal testimony that's come out in recent decades — from children molested by teachers, by Scout leaders, by priests at native residential schools, by parents and other relatives — certainly suggests that child sex abuse has been far from uncommon, right up through the puritanical forties and fifties, when Lucy and Ricky Ricardo slept in separate beds on TV.

So even in its heyday, the walled garden of childhood wasn't able to protect children from being sexually exploited by adults. In a society where children have no power and are viewed as the property of adults in other ways, it shouldn't really be surprising that some people abuse that power and treat kids as objects to be used for their own amusement and satisfaction. If anything, keeping children in a state of ignorance about sex may actually make them more vulnerable to being abused. The sexual frankness of the past couple of decades has meant that child sex abuse is finally being talked about openly, and that children are learning that they have the right to say "No" to adults. Yet so highly charged is the whole discussion around children and sex that, when Canada's child pornography law was struck down in the late nineties, condemned for being too vaguely worded and open to misinterpretation, right-wing politicians accused anyone who supported the court's decision of being in *favor* of kiddie porn.

The real question may be whether all our frantic efforts to maintain children's enforced ignorance make any sense in a world where kids *already know.* One of the most bitingly satirical — but all too accurate — portrayals of our cultural confusion and hypocrisy about sex is found in *South Park,* the notorious animated series about eight-year-olds in a Colorado town. One of the things that made the show so shocking when it first aired in 1997 was the way it frankly acknowledged the fall of the walled garden. Dirty words? Epithets like "crack whore?" Necrophilia? Eight-year-old Stan, Kyle, Cartman and Kenny have heard and (not quite) seen it all. But none of this makes them any more genuinely knowledgeable or sophisticated — or any less clueless about the real mechanics of sex — than their peers. When Chef, the character voiced by soul singer Isaac Hayes, serenades them with lascivious songs about "making sweet love all night long" in the school cafeteria, they react with dull-eyed bewilderment. They have only the barest glimmer of what he's talking about. One of the running jokes of *South Park* is how much the kids *think* they know, as opposed to how little they actually do know. In one episode, Cartman announces to the other boys that he's more mature than they are because "I got my period!"

It's interesting that Chef, the only adult who is frank and open about sex, is in many ways *South Park's* most moral character. He's the only one who isn't totally self-absorbed, who actually watches out for the kids' welfare, who talks *to* them rather than at them. Chef is who the kids go to when they want honest answers to their questions. ("Children," he sighs when the boys ask him to tell them what a lesbian is. "Don't your parents explain *anything* to you?")

So what *do* we do about kids and sex in the media? Do we just throw up our hands, say anything goes, and let seven-year-olds watch hardcore porn films? Of course not. But the boundaries have shifted: today's kids are growing up in a much more open sexual environment. It's a reality we have to deal with.

Not long ago I watched the film *Pleasantville* on video with several ten- and eleven- year-old girls. The movie shows how a couple of hip, sexually experienced teenagers from the nineties get transported into a fifties-era sitcom and shake up the placid, asexual, black-and-white lives of the old show's characters. Soon the Pleasantville teens start going all the way with a vengeance on lovers' lane, and even the uptight adult characters get into the spirit of erotic discovery. I don't think I've ever seen a more "graphic" sex scene than the one in which the housewife played (exquisitely) by Joan Allen discovers the joy of masturbation when she's in the bathtub. Though there's no nudity and all we see is her face, as her voice rises to an orgasmic crescendo, the camera cuts to a shot of a the tree outside the house, which suddenly bursts into brilliant red flames.

As I watched the scene with the girls, I waited for their reaction. But there were no cries of, "Ewwwww!" They didn't turn away or hide their eyes as I'd seen them do before during mushy kissing scenes. There was something about the movie's theme of innocence and discovery, a delicacy about its treatment of sexual awakening that seemed to strike just the right note with them. "Did you understand what was going on in that scene?" I asked them later. They firmly replied "Yes" in unison. It was clear that they didn't want me to ask any more. And that nothing more needed to be said anyway.

When Bad Things Happen to Good People

The whole point of the walled garden of childhood is to keep kids from knowing about things we don't want them to know about. But of course it also has a protective function: we're trying to keep them from things we believe will harm them. As I've tried to show in this chapter, there's considerable confusion about what's truly harmful to children and what isn't, a confusion that's even more pronounced in our attitudes toward violence, the third member of the Unholy Trinity. Adult anxieties about violence spring from a positive impulse to protect children from the painful realities of life — death, suffering, cruelty. However, the idea of special protection for children brings with it a tendency to go too far, to present children with an idealized, sugar-coated version of reality. This sentimentalized view of childhood is a middle-class legacy of the Victorian era, one that still exerts a powerful influence on contemporary attitudes.

One way this has manifested itself is in the debate about fairy tales. Adults have long been profoundly uncomfortable with the various painful realities that are the very stuff of fairy tales — orphaned children, cruel stepmothers, and murderous ogres. Though in recent decades there have been complaints about sexism and racial stereotypes in fairy tales, the most common charge against them is that they're too grim and violent for children. Ever since these stories were collected and popularized in the early 19th century by the Grimm brothers, Charles Perrault and other writers, many educators and child experts have argued that fairy tales are unhealthy for children, and that they should instead be brought up on a diet of realistic stories that teach clear moral lessons.

Others have challenged this view, notably the late child psychiatrist Bruno Bettelheim. In his influential book, *The Uses of Enchantment,* Bettelheim puts forth the idea that fairy tales are an important part of the child's struggle to make meaning of life and its difficulties. Bettelheim believed that the dramatic vitality of fairy tales gives them a powerful appeal that can't be matched by moral tales. He argues that children instinctively understand and appreciate their deep folk wisdom — an acknowledgement that life is painful and inherently unfair, and that bad things happen, even to good people. We'd rather they didn't find these things out, but it's not something we can prevent. Children *do* suffer pain, both from major traumas like abuse or the death of a parent, and from the more mundane difficulties of daily life. And with their heightened sensitivity and lack of life experience, even "small" problems can seem much larger and more painful to children than they might to adults. Bettelheim argued that fairy tales can help by allowing them to face life's difficulties and overcome — in fantasy at least — their worst fears of abandonment and loss.

It's not that we should ignore our protective instincts, or reject the belief that certain kinds of knowledge are too painful for children. That's exactly what the happily-ever-after fairy tale ending is for, corny as it so often seems to adults. Because what children *do* need to be shielded from is not the painful realities of life so much as a sense of hopelessness about them. Some kinds of stories really are too "adult" — too in-your-face, too cynical, too intellectual, too nihilistic, too overwhelming. Kids lack many of the inner filters that grown-ups have to process this kind of material, and writers for young children in particular have to walk a fine line to avoid going into territory that's too painful for their audiences to accept. This is one area where age really *does* matter, where the level of a child's cognitive and emotional development really does have a bearing.

But even here things are shifting: when *Jurassic Park* came out in 1993, a flurry of media articles warned parents that some experts felt the movie was too frightening for children under eight. But what did they know? Kids as young as four and five flocked to see the movie, and wild horses (or marauding dinosaurs) couldn't have kept them away. Things were different in my house, though. Ivy, who was six at the time, made it clear that no matter what her friends were doing, she wasn't interested. From the TV ads and movie trailers, she'd decided it looked way too scary. But a year or so later, she was eager to see *Fly Away Home,* a critically acclaimed film about a girl whose parents are divorced. The movie opens with a horrifying scene of a car crash, which the heroine survives but which kills her mother. The girl then goes to live with her father and gets caught up in his plans to train a gaggle of orphaned geese to migrate south for the first time.

As we watched, I was palpably aware of Ivy's extreme distress during that opening scene. The rest of the movie unfolded as a feel-good story, but I don't think she bought into it, and the film's happy ending could only do so much to allay the powerful emotions that first scene had churned up in her psyche. *Fly Away Home* did very well at the box office and was praised by many reviewers as a superior family film, but I thought it was too much for my seven-year-old. I think it relates to a certain folk wisdom prevalent in fairy tales, which dictates that the death of the mother — *the* primal trauma in the psychic universe of the fairy tale — should happen "offstage," before the story begins. This is as true of the best-known tales, "Cinderella" and "Snow White" for example, as it is of lesser-known ones like "Donkeyskin" and "The Goose-Girl." Even when such a death occurs in the course of a story, as in the modern children's classic *Charlotte's Web* (Charlotte the spider being the closest thing to a mother that Wilbur the pig has), it takes a writer with E.B. White's sensitivity to know how much sorrow is too much for his young readers. White is careful to leave them hope for the future in the birth of Charlotte's daughters the following summer.

But the muted violence of fairy tales, even the traumatic death scene in *Fly Away Home,* isn't what parents are concerned about these days. They're worried about violence with a capital "V" — in video games, in movies and on TV. Their concerns have given rise to an anti-violence movement that's dominated media coverage and public discussion about children over the past two decades. It's become even more virulent in the wake of incidents like the 1999 high-school shootings in Littleton, Colorado. But in many ways this anti-violence crusade is just one more battle in the long-running culture war between adults and children.

Storming the Walled Garden: The Kid-Culture Wars

If it's true that childhood is a kind of walled garden, then it shouldn't surprise us that children try to poke through the wall every chance they get. Where there are secrets, kids will try to uncover them, simply because it's their nature to want to know. In fact, it's precisely *because* this knowledge is kept secret that it becomes so highly charged for kids. The forbidden fruit is invariably the most appealing.

In fact, the history of this past century is one of culture wars between adults and children. Each new medium brings new forms of entertainment that children crave access to, and which adults try to deny them. Early in the 20th century, kids flocked to the movies. Saturday matinee became a major children's pastime, as well as a source of adult anxiety. Large groups of children crammed together in dark movie houses, taking in the marvelous new medium, away from their parents' watchful eyes. Right from those earliest days, there was the now-familiar litany of concerns: Adults were worried about sex and violence in movies. They didn't think films were "educational" enough, and feared that watching them would stunt kids' intellectual growth and destroy their imaginations. Just as television and computer games were feared and blamed in the nineties, so in the past did public anxiety and political expediency seize upon children's cinema diet as a source of society's ills.

A good deal of the content of films in those early days was undeniably what we would consider adult. Many of the Hollywood films of the twenties dealt with frankly sexual themes, and though these were hardly the stuff of kids' matinees, pressures built through the decade to clean up the movies. With the establishment of the

Production Code in the early thirties, the anything-goes atmosphere came to an end. From the mid-thirties through to the late sixties, the Production Code forbade overt suggestions of sexuality in Hollywood films, until the sexual revolution ushered in a new freedom and "adult" themes and frank language reappeared in films. But during the three decades the Production Code was in full force, it was as if the whole of North American society lived in the walled garden of childhood, at least as far as the movies were concerned.

Meanwhile, in the fifties, the Saturday matinee was dying out as a children's pastime and a new form of kids' entertainment began to set off alarm bells with adults. Comic books grew out of the comic strips in daily newspapers, and first began to appear as free-standing booklets in the forties. Though the early books encompassed a number of story genres — the domestic humor of Dagwood and Blondie, the high-school hijinks of Archie and Veronica — it was the horror, action and true-crime comics with titles like *Tales from the Crypt* and *Two-Fisted Tales* that became wildly popular. Psychiatrist Frederic Wertham condemned them, claiming they were a major cause of the rise in juvenile delinquency in the United States. Wertham's 1953 book, *Seduction of the Innocent,* sparked a moral crusade against comics that culminated in the set-up of a special U.S. Senate subcommittee to examine the alleged link between comics and juvenile crime. As it did with Hollywood films, the inevitable clampdown came in the form of a code, which placed severe restrictions on the subject matter and imagery in the books, driving many of the horror and true-crime comics off the market altogether.

Adults were able to shore up the walled garden as far as children's exposure to movies and comic books was concerned. But as I've noted earlier, it was television that proved its ultimate downfall, television that has profoundly and irrevocably altered the landscape of modern childhood. As far back as 1961, Federal Communications Commission Chairman Newton Minow sounded the alarm about TV's effect on children in his famous "vast wasteland" speech.

Noting that the average American child was spending as much time in front of a TV set as in school, Minow warned that children's lives were no longer being molded primarily by home, school and church, but by a new "fourth great influence" — television.

Of course, what concerned Minow about television back then wasn't sex or bad language. Television in its early years was, if anything, more squeaky-clean than the movies during the Production Code era. Even Lucy and Ricky Ricardo had to be shown sleeping in separate beds on *I Love Lucy*. But, though violent programs were one of Minow's major targets in his "wasteland" speech, it took another two decades before the issue of children and TV violence began to claim a major part of the political landscape. The catalyst for the first major wave of the anti-TV-violence crusade in the mid-eighties was the debut of the animated series *Teenage Mutant Ninja Turtles*. Though previous kids' shows had featured the military combat of *GI Joe*, the falling anvils of *Bugs Bunny*, and the slapstick mayhem of *Roadrunner*, the look and feel of *Ninja Turtles* was something new, combining jokey humor with the thrill of action-adventure. The series about four oversized turtle crime-fighters had its roots in an underground comic, which itself was a send-up of comic-book superheroes. Unlike GI Joe, the Ninja Turtles didn't use guns or weaponry, but overpowered the enemy with martial arts moves that were widely imitated on playgrounds across North America. The *Ninja Turtles* craze was the first to usher in the now-familiar charges of copycat violence.

Though it was just moving out into the mainstream, the issue of TV violence and its effect on children had been bubbling away in academia for some time. Beginning in the early seventies, social scientist Leonard Eron identified violent TV programs as a major cause of aggressive behavior in children. Eron's long-term studies of children's TV-viewing habits have provided some of the core texts for the anti-TV-violence movement. He claimed that his research showed a cause-and-effect relationship between TV violence and aggressive behavior that's as well established as the link between cigarette smoking and lung cancer. Another major academic figure in the anti-violence crusade is George Gerbner. The dean of the Annenberg School for Communication at the University of Pennsylvania, Gerbner is well known as the developer of the so-called violence index, a method of rating TV programs by tallying up the frequency of violent acts. Though widely cited and used in academic studies of TV violence, this method has drawn criticism for its disregard of context, as well as its failure to distinguish between slapstick cartoon mayhem and more realistic depictions of violence. But many anti-violence crusaders believe, along with Gerbner, that cartoons are the worst offenders, because they depict, as he puts it, "happy violence" or "violence without consequences."

Over time, critics of TV violence have moved from a simple monkey-see, monkey-do causal connection to the more sophisticated desensitization theory, which holds that exposure to fictional violence causes children to became numb to the real-life kind. An even more sophisticated cause-and-effect theory has been proposed by David Grossman, a former lieutenant-colonel in the U.S. Army. In his 1999 book, *Stop Teaching Our Kids to Kill,* Grossman focuses much of his attention on violent video games. He argues that they provide an almost military-style training in the mechanics of killing. According to Grossman, kids playing games like Doom develop a conditioned response similar to that of soldiers, who train for combat by firing at human-shaped targets on a shooting range. Still another idea that has come to hold wide currency is what Gerbner calls the "mean world syndrome," by which frequent viewers of violent TV shows come to believe that society at large is more violent than it actually is. The combined effect of these theories has been the creation of a climate in which the general public has eagerly embraced the idea that television is a major cause — if not *the* major cause — of violence in real life.

The crusade against TV violence moved into a new phase in the mid-nineties with the debut of *Mighty Morphin Power Rangers.* This series about five teenagers who can transform themselves or "morph" into aliens with superhero powers was an instant hit with kids worldwide. Like *Teenage Mutant Ninja Turtles, Power Rangers* was rooted in Asian martial-arts traditions, and featured stylized, choreographed combat scenes, as well as vaguely new-age elements like the power animals or "zords," which the Power Rangers summoned to help them in battle. The show was basically a nineties' variation on the old *Superman* theme, but with a number of stylistic twists, due to its origins in Japanese TV. Adults in North America were particularly disturbed by the show's throbbing, high-energy rock score, which pumped up the adrenaline of the combat sequences.

Mighty Morphin Power Rangers had only been on the air for a few weeks when the first complaints about kids copying the actions while on school playgrounds began to surface in the fall of 1994. Almost immediately, the show became the focus of near-hysteria worldwide. Canada became the first country to ban it when, after receiving a handful of complaints from parents, the country's broadcast regulation agency ordered stations to pull it off the air. In Sweden, *Power Rangers* was named as the catalyst for a case of copycat violence involving two boys who beat up a five-year-old girl. The show was also linked to the sensational murder of six-year-old James Bulger by two eleven-year-old boys in Britain.

With its powerful rhetoric and simplistic analysis, the TV violence issue was ripe for political exploitation. In the U.S., President Bill Clinton made it one of the touchstones of his family-values platform, and Keith Spicer, then head of Canada's broadcast regulatory agency, adopted the anti-TV-violence issue as a personal crusade. Spicer threatened to block the cable signals of U.S. stations beaming *Power Rangers* into Canada. He also threw his support behind development of the V-chip, a made-in-Canada screening device that could be programmed to block out programs with violence or other objectionable material. President Clinton soon got on the V-chip bandwagon, too, lauding it as the solution to the problem of TV violence, because it relied on parental discretion rather than state censorship. As Spicer enthused, the beauty of the V-chip was that it would "make parents into censors."

Most people assumed, understandably enough, that the "V" stood for violence. But the V-chip's inventor, British Columbia engineer Tim Collings, meant it to stand for viewer-control. (What the V-chip is really about, of course, is parent-control, because in this case the actual viewers are the kids.) It quickly became clear that there was more than just violence on many parents' minds. The explosion of cable and the dawn of the multi-channel universe were ushering in a new era of permissiveness. The nineties saw a gradual loosening of restrictions at the major TV networks, as they tried to fend off stiff competition from an ever-growing pool of specialty channels. Language and overtly sexual content that would have been unthinkable only a few years earlier became standard TV fare. Parents complained that even popular sitcoms such as *Friends* — with its penis jokes and casual references to "doing it" — were bringing the new permissiveness right into the prime-time family-viewing hours.

Some of the movement's leaders fought to keep the focus on TV violence. Keith Spicer, for example, stressed that he thought violence was the real culprit and said that TV needed *more* sex, not less. Parents of all political stripes weren't buying that line, though. Despite the experts' protestations, for parents the battle wasn't just about TV violence but rather the whole ball of wax: the Unholy Trinity of sex, violence and profanity that was flooding the airwaves and corrupting their children. Besides, it was becoming abundantly clear that the ratings system being developed for use with the V-chip wasn't going to target just violence, but all kinds of objectionable content.

Toward the end of the nineties, the anti-TV-violence crusade began to run out of steam. In the U.S., President Bill Clinton's advocacy of the V-chip became worthless as his moral authority plummeted in the wake of the Lewinsky sex scandal. The V-chip itself became like the proverbial check in the mail — always promised, never quite arriving. Plagued by a series of technical glitches and marketing difficulties, the momentum to bring the V-chip to market slowed down to a crawl, and there was little indication that parents would actually use it, when (and if) it became available. After all the sound and fury, by the end of the decade, children's television looked pretty much like it did at the beginning: plenty of superhero cartoons, action-adventure series and falling-anvil slapstick. Even *Power Rangers* was back on the air, in not one but two separate spin-off series.

In the vacuum left by the too-long-delayed V-chip, anti-violence crusaders felt they could claim at least a partial victory with the adoption of an age-based ratings system for television. But the fact is, as in the case of movies, TV ratings have very little impact on kids' real-world viewing habits. *South Park* is rated TV-M (18+ in the Canadian system), meaning it shouldn't be seen by viewers younger than eighteen. Yet kids aged ten to fifteen named it their second-favorite show, after *The Simpsons,* in a 1999 Toronto survey. The researchers professed surprise at the result, but they shouldn't have been. The multi-channel universe, the triumph of the VCR, even cultural changes like the shift to later bedtimes for kids — all these things render the whole notion of age-based ratings increasingly irrelevant for television.

If anything signaled the death knell of the crusade, it was the runaway success of *South Park.* The series premiered on the U.S. Comedy Central network in the spring of 1997. Critics were scandalized by its relentless assault on good taste and political correctness, but the fact that *South Park* was safely tucked away on a cable network probably minimized the public outcry. When Global, a cross-Canada network, picked up the show in the fall of 1997, I figured it was only a matter of time before the sputters of outrage began, even though it was running at the kid-unfriendly hour of midnight on Fridays. Surely the country that banned *Power Rangers* wouldn't stand for a program that featured a hunk of talking feces, not to mention the grisly death, week after week, of one of the main characters — played for laughs! Shades of George Gerbner's happy violence!

But the public outcry over *South Park* was decidedly underwhelming, even when the show moved to a prime-time slot on Canada's Comedy Network in 1998. So why did *South Park* get off scot-free, when the (comparatively) bland *Power Rangers* had stirred up such a fierce outcry only a few years earlier? Several factors came into play. For one thing, *South Park* is a slippery kind of entity. It doesn't feature the karate-kicking action-adventure of *Power Rangers* — aside from the weekly demise of Kenny, the show has almost no scenes of violence. What it does have is lots of nasty insults, extremely un-subtle sexual innuendo and infantile, gross humor. It may be that the genius of *South Park* lies in its ability to smash so many taboos without actually violating broadcasting standards or breaking any laws. Indeed, when they get around to watching the show, parents often can't pin down just what it is that's so objectionable about it. They just know they don't want their kids to watch it. Part of the reason may be that the show's humor hits a bit too close to home. Despite the fact that media reports invariably play up the scatological aspects of South Park, there's also a sharp satirical intelligence behind much of the writing. Witness this exchange between eight-year-old Stan and his mother about his parents' pending divorce:

"Stanley, you know you're the most important thing to me."
"Then get back together with dad for me."
"Now, Stanley, you know when I say that, what I mean is you're the most important thing after me, my happiness and my new romance."
"Oh."

South Park's creators, Trey Parker and Matt Stone, also managed to deflect criticism with their insistence that even though the show is *about* kids, it isn't *for* kids. It ran on an adult network, Comedy Central, during the evening rather than in the usual kids' time-slots like Saturday morning or after school. Yet despite Parker's and

Stone's protestations, it quickly became obvious to media observers that children as young as seven and eight were watching — and loving — *South Park.* This was hardly surprising. A show about kids, drawn in a crude style, with funny voices and lots of fart jokes — and they thought they were going to keep kids from watching it? One can only reply, in true late-nineties style, well, *duh.* Even the ones who couldn't stay up late or watch it on video knew all about the show from talking to friends who could. *South Park* also became an instant merchandising phenomenon, with "I Killed Kenny" and the ubiquitous image of Cartman on T-shirts, accompanied by the inevitable debates about whether or not kids should be allowed to wear them to school.

Though many parents and media watchdog groups continued to fight the good fight against the Unholy Trinity, by the turn of the millennium it was clear that they were engaged in little more than a rearguard action. But not everyone was caving in to the new permissiveness. The Christian Right continues to fight the tide, using tools like the aforementioned CAPalert Website, which rates films on something it calls the WISDOM scale: for Wanton violence, Impudence, Sex (including homosexuality), Drugs-and-alcohol, Offence to God and — last but not least — Murder. (CAPalert's reviewer declared the movie *South Park: Bigger, Longer and Uncut* to be "straight from the smoking pit of Hell.") At the same time, some right-wing Christians are coming around to the idea that "if you can't lick 'em, join 'em." They are directing their efforts toward creating and promoting their own forms of feel-good pop culture. A major success story in the children's market was *Veggie Tales,* a series of videos featuring animated tomatoes, cukes and other vegetables who sing, dance and teach moral lessons from the Bible. An even greater breakthrough in 1999 was the phenomenal success of the apocalypse-themed *Left Behind* books, which broke onto *The New York Times* bestseller list, followed by a big-budget movie that its creators trumpeted as the genre's equivalent to *Star Wars.*

Much as fundamentalists have given up on the public school system and turned their energies toward establishing their own back-to-basics charter schools, the success of religious-themed ventures will encourage them to concentrate on doing more of the same in the entertainment arena. Because even social conservatives know that, culturally, the battle against the Unholy Trinity is over. Neil Postman is right. We *are* going back to the Middle Ages.

GOING MEDIEVAL:
THE NEW ALL-AGES CULTURE

"REAL MATURE, BRADLEY!"

That's a stock phrase from *Stickin' Around,* a witty animated series about a couple of kids who just happen to be stick-figures. The girl, Stacey, says it to her pal Bradley whenever he does something dumb (which is several times an episode). She delivers the line in a droll, eye-rolling, but not nasty tone, the way friends like to razz one another. For a while it became something of a pet phrase around our house.

Recently, when I caught an episode of *Stickin' Around* after not having seen it for a while, it struck me that "Real mature, Bradley!" was an updated version of a phrase that was around when I was growing up. "Act your age!" my friends and I used to chide one another when one of us did something stupid.

It's a phrase you don't hear much anymore. I wonder if that's partly because we're not sure we know what it means now. What does it mean, really, to "act your age"? It's a question that has entered the cultural zeitgeist in the past few decades, popping up in the Hollywood films *Big* (a grown man becomes a child), *Jack* (a child becomes a grown man) and *Baby Geniuses* (children are smarter than adults).

So much of modern life is organized around what sociologist Joshua Meyerowitz refers to in *No Sense of Place* as "the myth of age-determinism": the idea that the only right way to carry out certain activities is to separate people by age. Leisure time, for example, is organized around two basic principles: the belief that adults and children have different tastes and amuse themselves in fundamentally different ways; and the related notion that most of the pastimes that appeal to adults aren't suitable for children — either because they're beyond kids' level of understanding, or because they're corrupting influences. So pronounced is this separation, that in many situations, the word adult has become a code for sexual content. Everybody knows, for example, that an adult video store is one that carries porn movies. But our preoccupation with age segregation and generational differences is, like the idea of childhood itself, a relatively recent historical development. Take schooling, for example. It took several centuries for the concept of separate classes — the practice of teaching pupils in homogenous groups divided according to age — to evolve. In the schools and universities of the Middle Ages, students of diverse ages — including both adults and youth — worked and learned together. Nowadays, of course, age segregation is the very foundation of Western-based education systems. We only dispense with it when necessary (as in the old one-room rural schoolhouses), and we rarely entertain the thought that things could or should be otherwise.

But in medieval life, generational "markers" — things that distinguished people according to age — were almost non-existent. As Philippe Ariès observes in *Centuries of Childhood,* children in European paintings of the Middle Ages were not depicted with any distinctively childlike characteristics, other than smaller size. They were essentially pint-size adults. It was only over the subsequent centuries that the more familiar (to us) pictures of children with appealing, cherub-like features began to appear with greater frequency. Similarly, Ariès notes the lack of differentiation between children's and adults' clothing back then: "As soon as the child abandoned his swaddling-band — the band of cloth that was wound tightly around his body in babyhood — he was dressed just like the other men and women of his class."[1] This lack of differentiation between adults' and children's styles of dress constitutes one of the centerpieces of Ariès' argument that childhood did not exist as a separate category of life in the medieval era. But by the 17th century, a particular children's costume with more precious qualities, setting it apart from adult styles of dress, appeared on the scene. In Ariès' view, this development "marked a very important date in the formation of the idea of childhood."[2]

This sharp distinction between the generations in style of dress carried right through the better part of the 20th century. When I was growing up, not only were you supposed to act your age, you were supposed to dress your age, too. Not any more. These days, the practice of dressing children in clothes meant just for them is rapidly becoming a thing of the past. From a fashion standpoint, at least, our kids have a lot in common with the miniature adults in the paintings cited by Ariès. This "uni-age" style of dress has developed gradually but inexorably over the past few decades; a trend pioneered, like so many others, by baby boomers who refuse to accept the dictates of age for themselves or for their children. As Michael Budman, one of the founders of Canada's boomer-friendly Roots clothing chain, told a Toronto *Globe and Mail* fashion reporter: "We don't like to see our kids dressed like clowns. When I grew up I only saw my dad in a sport coat and tie. Now, my son and daughter and I are dressed similarly." Generation-blurring has become the watchword in the fashion industry, as fortysomethings wear jeans, eleven-year-olds wear spaghetti-strap dresses, and pretty much everybody can wear cargo pants from GAP. We're evolving into a society in which age distinctions mean less and less.

This trend also applies to the very ways we amuse ourselves, and it's one more way in which our culture is becoming more and more like the Middle Ages. In the medieval world, adults unabashedly took part in what many people today would consider childish games of hide-and-seek and hand-clapping rhymes. One famous medieval

Book of Hours shows an entire village of men, women and children engaging in a rousing snowball fight. Much of village life revolved around the great seasonal feasts like Midsummer Day and Twelfth Night, with pageants and festivals that typically went on for days at a stretch. These festivals were all-ages events, conducted, according to Ariès, in the fashion of a "collective game which mobilized the whole of society and brought all age groups together."[3] Young and old alike would gather to hear the tales of itinerant storytellers and watch performances by travelling troupes of players. (One important difference, of course, was that they didn't have the great gulf between performer and audience that prevails in our star-driven, celebrity-obsessed world.) Of all our contemporary holidays, Hallowe'en (known throughout medieval Europe by its Celtic name *Samhain*) perhaps comes closest to reproducing this broadly partici-patory character. Both adults and children dress up in costumes, going out in the night to partake in communal revelry. Trick-or-treating, now considered a children's activity, is a contemporary ver-sion of the ancient custom of mummering carried out by adult men (a practice which still survives in Newfoundland and other outposts of traditional Celtic culture).

In recent years, newer celebrations are carrying on this all-ages trend. For example, New Year's Eve has traditionally been a night when adults get dressed up, go out for a fancy dinner and stay out late. With the growing popularity of First Night street festivals in North American cities, many parents are choosing to spend the big night with their children instead of leaving them with babysitters.

In the centuries following the Middle Ages, the development of widespread literacy and the rise of an educated middle class fos-tered the notion of a more intellectual, "highbrow" sphere of culture for adults that was beyond children's understanding or ability to appreciate. But the development of mass media changed all that: increasingly, popular culture is all-ages culture. Nowadays, child-hood and adulthood are blending into one another in ways

Westerners haven't seen for the past 500 years. For example, kids, teens and grown-ups alike flock to indoor playgrounds like Sgt. Splatter's Paintball and high-tech funhouses like the Playdium chain to enjoy the exact same games. Through the nineties, the whole notion of family entertainment was undergoing a sea-change, too, as kids flocked to movies and watched TV shows intended for adult audiences, while traditional "kiddie" fare like animation began to attract more and more adults.

Growing Up and Dumbing-Down

When the original *Star Wars* was released in 1977, its chief target audience was ten- to twelve-year-old boys, and creator George Lucas thought it would be a modestly successful kids' movie. Instead, *Star Wars* brought about a revolution in the the movie business, as it ushered in the era of the blockbuster and almost singlehandedly led, in the judgement of many critics, to a massive dumbing-down of American culture. The wider cultural significance of the *Star Wars* phenomenon continued with *The Phantom Menace* in 1999, as the frenzy around the film's release became emblematic of the ever-widening swath of pop culture shared by adults and children. Nostalgic baby-boomers took their kids to see it, and spoke of bonding through their shared interest in the film.

Of course, the *Star Wars* movies are nothing if not straight-ahead family films, with their old-fashioned storytelling and good vs. evil plotlines. But Lucas' phenomenal success notwithstanding, when it comes to the traditional family film, no studio has the stunning record that Walt Disney established with his. Disney's pioneering work in animated features began with the release of *Snow White* in 1937, and continued through the forties and fifties with hits such as *Cinderella* and *Lady and the Tramp.* But in the sixties and seventies, Disney's animation division fell on hard times. With the new sexual frankness and graphic violence in films (think of *Bonnie and Clyde* and

Last Tango in Paris), there no longer seemed to be a market for movies with general, all-ages appeal.

That began to change in the late eighties with the release of *The Little Mermaid,* the studio's first animated feature in more than a decade. With its Caribbean-flavored musical score and the zany antics of characters like Sebastian the singing crab, the film was an immediate hit with kids. But to their amazement, Disney executives found that it appealed to adults as well. Almost overnight, *The Little Mermaid* had made Disney movies, as one company executive told *Entertainment Weekly,* "okay for grown-ups." The film also laid down the formula for the fabulously successful string of animated features put out by the company through the nineties. To keep adults interested, the films offered tuneful, reasonably sophisticated musical scores (which reached a pinnacle with the Oscar-winning *Beauty and the Beast* in 1991) and hip, knowing pop culture references, played to especially great effect by Robin Williams' fast-talking genie in *Aladdin.* For the kids, the movies rely on the tried-and-true appeal of traditional fairy-tale narratives, jazzed up with cute animal critters and lots of slapstick humor. Disney's winning streak reached its apex in 1994 with *The Lion King,* the sixth-highest-grossing film of all time. (The company subsequently went on to revitalize live musical theater with the phenomenally successful stage version, still selling out on Broadway more than three years after its opening.)

Disney's string of successes began to taper off, though. 1998's *Hercules* was a dud, at least by Disney standards, and though *Pocahontas* and *Mulan* did better, their more serious and female-centered storylines kept them from achieving blockbuster success. Around the same time, the company faced a new problem — competition — as other studios tried to scramble onto the family-film gravy train and began to borrow the Disney formula. The late nineties saw the start of what was termed the Animation Wars. The studio's chief rival was Dreamworks, helmed by Steven Spielberg and former Disney head honcho Jeffrey Katzenberg, whose drive to make his mark in animation was fuelled by deep personal resentment toward his old employer. (After leaving Disney, Katzenberg sued the studio for a portion of the profits from *The Lion King* and other animated hits. He eventually won a multi-million-dollar settlement.) The rivalry between the two studios came to a head in 1998 with the release, within weeks of one another, of two similarly themed animated features — *Antz* from Dreamworks and Disney's *A Bug's Life*.

While these two duked it out, other studios lost their shirts on mostly forgettable fare like Paramount's *Anastasia* and Warner's *Quest for Camelot*. These features were done with lush, expensive, hand-drawn animation, big-name voice talent, and the by-now-mandatory formula elements like comical sidekicks and light pop-music scores. But they lacked the narrative punch of the best Disney movies and did tepid business in what was turning into an increasingly crowded market. Toward Christmas of 1998, the Animation Wars took a new turn as Dreamworks broke from the Disney formula with the release of *The Prince of Egypt*. The sweeping biblical epic had no cute talking animals, and was marketed without the standard merchandising tie-ins. According to *Entertainment Weekly,* Katzenberg told his team he intended to take the high road, that with *Prince of Egypt* "there's not going to be dolls and a Moses burger and a burning-bush nightlight." But while Katzenberg's bid to have the film treated as serious, adult entertainment led to a largely favorable reaction from critics, *Prince of Egypt* didn't connect with audiences in the way he'd hoped. (Though I liked the film, I found it curiously muted in its storytelling, given that the biblical story is so inherently dramatic. Much screen time is given over to a contrived rivalry between Moses and his stepbrother Ramses, for example, while the seven plagues are whittled down to two.)

Well before Dreamworks entered the fray, however, Disney had struck out in new directions through its partnership with pioneering computer-animation studio Pixar. Their first major joint venture was the 1995 hit *Toy Story*. The film was a dramatic break with the studio's tried-and-true formula: the story was original and contemporary, not based on a fairy tale; plus, the computer-generated images gave *Toy Story* a whole different look and feel from the studio's well-known classics. But Disney's gamble paid off handsomely, as *Toy Story's* broad cross-generational appeal rivalled the breakthrough that *The Little Mermaid* had achieved a decade earlier. All across the country, film audiences were populated not just with kids, but also with grown-ups drawn by the film's fresh sensibility and edgy — for Disney, at least — humor. Four years later, *Toy Story 2* built upon its predecessor's success. Originally slated for a direct-to-video release, the sequel was a huge box-office hit in theaters and found favor with critic Roger Ebert, who was won over by its funny, touching tale of toys grappling with mortality, and included it on his ten-best list for 1999. No less a culture maven than Susan Sontag declared that, in her opinion, *Toy Story 2* was a better film than the Oscar-winning drama *American Beauty*.

The blessing of these critics has helped bring a whole new level of artistic respectability to big-screen animation. In many ways, live-action family films face an even more difficult task, that of trying to please audiences of all ages without the unhinged freedom of animation or the built-in kid-appeal of adorable cartoon characters. To date, no film has achieved that balancing act with greater success — both artistic and financial — than *Babe*. When it was released in 1995, the film was hailed as a sophisticated, witty fable with dashes of pathos and even tragedy — especially in the dark, daring opening sequence when the little pig, Babe, narrowly escapes being sent to the slaughterhouse. Many critics instantly recognized that this was a whole new breed of family film, with qualities that called to mind some of the timeless children's classics such as E.B. White's *Charlotte's Web*. And *Babe* was able to draw on the remarkable achievements in special-effects and animatronics technology to create its seamless and utterly believable world of all-talking, all-singing barnyard animals. The result was a true work of cinematic art that transcended the existing categories of children's and adult's entertainment. In 1995, *Babe* became one of only a handful of family films ever to receive an Oscar nomination for Best Picture (*The Wizard of Oz* was another).

But the fate of the sequel was a cautionary tale, illustrating what a fine line these films must walk. Even before its release in 1999, *Babe: Pig in the City* suffered from negative word of mouth as being too grim for kids. And it is certainly true that the film has a darker quality than its precedessor. It is set in an unnamed city designed to recall early classics of German expressionism, like Fritz Lang's *Metropolis.* And there are some truly frightening scenes — for example, one where Babe is being chased by a vicious pit bull. In one of the film's wittiest sequences, the dog ultimately becomes Babe's protector. "What the pig says," he tells the other animals, "goes."

The fear that this sequel was too bleak resulted in audiences staying away in droves, and reviewers and industry insiders alike castigated the director, George Miller, for departing from the sunny world of the original. Nevertheless, there were a handful of critics, including the late Gene Siskel, who embraced *Babe: Pig in the City,* hailing it as a deeper, more artistically ambitious film than its predecessor. Siskel put it at the top of his last ten-best list before his death in 1999. But the perception that *Babe* wasn't suitable for children proved disastrous at the box office. (I personally urged parents and kids who'd stayed away because of the negative buzz to rent it once it came out on video. Every one of them loved it, and not one parent reported back to me that they found the movie too grim.)

While children's films were, in a sense, growing up and becoming more sophisticated, another trend — kids watching movies meant for adult audiences — was having an even wider impact. In the nineties, there came to be a much wider pool of films that parents and kids could comfortably (or not so comfortably) sit through together. And kids themselves were eager to see more grown-up fare. Two Julia Roberts vehicles, *My Best Friend's Wedding* and *Notting Hill,* were huge hits with young girls, and preteens of both sexes flocked to *Men in Black* and *Scream* — pictures that a decade earlier would have been deemed too scary or violent. The astounding success of *There's Something about Mary* showed just how far this trend of kids seeing adult films had developed. Once it garnered a reputation as the supreme gross-out movie of all time, kids were determined to find a way to see it, R-rating or no R-rating.

What the film industry was learning through the nineties was that all the old assumptions about age-specific marketing were breaking down. Kids have always tended to identify upward, aping the tastes of the group just a bit older than they are. But the whole process has accelerated. Younger kids nowadays won't waste their time on what they think of as kiddie-fare; they're interested in seeing the same movies as teens and grown-ups. In fact, producers admit that they actively seek out a PG-rating for their family films, because it has more cachet and draws more kids than a sappy-sounding G. Another key element of Hollywood's interest in courting younger audiences can be summed up by a single phrase: repeat business. When adults see a film they like, they might go back to see it again, perhaps even twice more. But kids' willingness to see their favorite movies repeatedly can spell the difference between mere box-office success and true blockbuster status. The outstanding example of this phenomenon is *Titanic,* the world-wide box-office champion. The film's release in 1998 was a collective event, one that kids clamored to be part of. The film's astounding success was also due in no small part to repeat viewings by teen and pre-teen girls, drawn by the story of doomed young lovers and the casting of idol Leonardo DiCaprio. There were reports of girls as young as six and seven going to see the movie dozens of times. Such was the kid-drawing power of *Titanic* that they were the major factor in the record ratings for the telecast of the 1998 Oscars: the Nielsen ratings showed that almost twice as many viewers in the two to eleven age bracket watched that year than had the year before. *Titanic* swept most of the major awards.

One welcome side-effect of the maturing of the family film is a change in the way kids themselves are portrayed. *The Sixth Sense,* one of the surprise hits of the late nineties, was a dark, disturbing thriller clearly aimed at adult audiences. But the film's trailer of young actor Haley Joel Osment whispering "I see dead people" was an irresistible draw for kids of all ages. And the ones who went to the movie saw more than a well-crafted ghost story. In Osment's tormented character they saw a real person, much like themselves, instead of the too-cute, smart-aleck kids who populate so many Hollywood movies. In the interplay between Osment and actor Bruce Willis' therapist, audiences were also treated to an unusually honest portrait of an adult–child relationship. In *The Sixth Sense* these two characters are portrayed as equals, working together to resolve a terrible dilemma. Far from being the all-knowing adult, the therapist is in as much pain and confusion as the child he's treating. The same goes for the film's depiction of a difficult but all-too-real parent–child relationship. Osment's mother, played by Toni Collette, is a harried and not very together woman. Her son's problems have pushed her to the brink. But at the film's most crucial moments, her best instincts kick in and she comes through for him. When he confides that the kids at school call him a freak, she looks him in the eye and tells him fiercely: "That's bullshit! Don't let anybody tell you that!" ("You said the s-word," the boy replies, in the movie's sly nod to our collective hang-up about kids and profanity — as if hearing the s-word wasn't the least of this kid's problems.)

Straddling the Generational Fence

The very same cultural trends that are redefining the family film are evident on TV. Since the earliest days of television, the early evening hours were regarded as a family-viewing time slot, while (slightly) more adult content was reserved for after 9 p.m., on the assumption that most kids were in bed by then (no longer a safe assumption, obviously). No single TV show has altered the tone of the family viewing hour more than *Friends.* The 2000 season premiere, for instance, consisted of three interlinked storylines: Chandler upset because he couldn't get it up with Monica, Joey teasing Rachel after he finds a soft-core porn novel in her bed, and Rachel and Ross contemplating a "bonus night" of no-strings, guilt-free sex. But right from the beginning, *Friends* was a big hit with kids. Pre-teens regularly cite the sitcom as one of their favorite shows in viewer surveys.

While the kids tune in to adult fare, plenty of grown-ups are tuning in to children's programming, to the point where it's become *de rigueur* for producers to add sophisticated humor to appeal to adult sensibilities. The Nickelodeon series, *Rugrats* — one of the highest rated cable shows on U.S. television — is a good example. It's about four diaper-clad babies, but it also has some wickedly satirical fun at their baby-boomer parents' expense. Some of the hipper kids' shows — Warners Bros.' *Animaniacs* and Nickelodeon's *PowerPuff Girls* come to mind — have developed cult followings among adults (not to mention the phenomenon of British ravers grooving on the Teletubbies). But there are still plenty of resolutely un-hip kids' shows that buck the trend, making no concessions to adult tastes — as the astounding persistence of *Barney and Friends* attests to.

Today's adult-friendly kids' shows have their antecedents in earlier trailblazers. *PeeWee's Playhouse,* a wildly original Saturday morning show, garnered a passionate adult following during its heyday in the late eighties. (It's more than a little ironic to recall that, only a few short years before the White House sex scandal, the star of *Pee-Wee's Playhouse,* Paul Reubens, was unceremoniously bounced from the air for the high crime of getting caught masturbating in an adult theater.) The grandaddy of all-ages kids' shows is unquestionably *Sesame Street,* which, for more than three decades, has been managing the canny feat of entertaining adults with pop-culture parodies and kids with cuddly Muppets like Elmo. From the show's earliest days, some critics have complained that a lot of the humor flies right over little kids' heads. But as far as *Sesame Street's* producers are concerned, it doesn't matter a whit that the show's youngest viewers don't have a clue that, say, "Monsterpiece Theater" is a send-up of PBS's venerable *Masterpiece Theatre,* because they're perfectly content to watch Cookie Monster (aka "Allistair Cookie") do his thing. One reason *Sesame Street* has so successfully straddled the generational fence may be that creator Jim Henson himself never worried much about whether his Muppets were for kids or adults. When Henson first started working in TV in the late fifties and early sixties, he put Kermit the Frog and other Muppets on grown-up entertainment like Ed Sullivan's variety program and Jack Paar's late-night talk show.

In fact, we're now seeing something of a return to the all-ages entertainment of that earlier era of TV, as whole households gather on Sunday evenings to watch *Who Wants to be a Millionaire*, much as they did in the fifties for *The Ed Sullivan Show*, as well as *The 64 Thousand Dollar Question* and other quiz shows. The creators of *Millionaire* were aware of the broad appeal of the concept right from the start and built it into the structure of the show. As host Regis Philbin told *Entertainment Weekly, Millionaire's* easier questions are included specifically with kids in mind, "so they'll feel they have a voice on the show." In 2000, the producers launched a new family edition, in which contestants could share the hot seat with one of their own kids (presumably, so that clueless parents could get help with questions about hip-hop artists and the like).

The one show that stands out as the epitome of all-ages entertainment is undoubtedly *The Simpsons.* Ever since it first hit the airwaves in 1989, this animated series has parlayed its signature mix of sitcom storytelling, visual slapstick, and rapid-fire pop culture references into a multilayered social satire. The particular genius of *The Simpsons* is that it's never defined itself as being for one age-group or another: it just is what it is, which is consistently, and often brilliantly, funny. It's been interesting to watch the evolution in the public's attitudes about the show. In its first few years on the air, *The Simpsons* was the show adults constantly pointed to as the symbol of all that was wrong with TV. The character of Bart, in particular, stuck in many grown-ups' craws: he was a bad influence, they complained, encouraging kids to act up, to use nasty insults like "Eat my shorts," to talk back to adults. (People tended to overlook the fact that lippy kids existed long before Bart Simpson. Of course, once the notorious *South Park* kids came along, Bart looked positively angelic in comparison.) But *The Simpsons* outlasted its naysayers. By the time it celebrated its tenth anniversary episode in 2000, the show had attained the status of a cultural icon, defining its times in much the same way as, say, *Father Knows Best* came to define the fifties sensibility. That same year, no less an arbiter of mainstream taste than *Time* magazine declared *The Simpsons* the best television series of the century.

Animated Adults

Between them, *The Simpsons* and Disney movies have ushered in a new era of respectability for animation, making it ready for adult prime time audiences. But animation's identity as kiddie entertainment is still fairly entrenched, thanks largely to the legacy of Uncle Walt himself. Back in the early days of big-screen animation, there were animators — like Max Fleischer, Chuck Jones and Tex Avery (creator of Bugs Bunny) — who worked with a more adult sensibility. But it was Walt Disney who laid down the template for the form and defined it as a children's genre, with the success of his first feature, *Snow White*. Even with the loftier ambitions of *Fantasia* in the forties, Disney found he couldn't break the mold he had created. Despite the film's classical score and high-art pretensions, *Fantasia's* dancing hippos and big-eyed, adorable fairies ensured that it would remain firmly identified as children's entertainment. Only recently, with the success of the revamped *Fantasia 2000*, have Disney's hopes for the original begun to bear fruit. Most critics still don't consider *Fantasia 2000* to be high art, but the film has certainly garnered a more adult-friendly identity, due in large part to its exploitation of the big-screen IMAX format.

But Disney-style animation is far from being the norm else-where in the world. Canada, for example, has forged a tradition of art animation, largely through the work of pioneering animator Norman MacLaren and his association with the National Film Board. And yet even MacLaren's best-known films (of which *Pas de Deux* is one) don't have the mass appeal of Disney films — they're almost painterly shorts on abstract themes, not feature-length vehicles for popular storytelling. But there are countries with popular forms of animation a la Disney — most notably Japan. Unlike American-style animation, *anime* (pronounced "an-ee-may"), as it's known in Japan, never had a kiddie reputation to live down. It's long been seen as a full-fledged popular art form in its own right, and as a medium for telling stories in any number of genres. There are virtually no subjects considered off-limits for anime. *Perfect Blue,* a psychological thriller about a pop singer stalked by a killer, was described by North American reviewers as "Hitchcockian" when it was released in 1999, and one critic hailed the epic *Grave of the Fireflies,* released the same year, as the *Schindler's List* of animation. There are anime features about such hard-hitting subjects as the dropping of the A-bomb on Hiroshima *(Barefoot Gen),* as well as the sadistic, graphically violent *Legend of the Overfiend.* There's even a whole notorious subgenre of hard-core porn.

In recent years, the popular appeal of Japanese anime has been moving it beyond mere cult status. The cyberpunk thriller *Ghost in the Shell* was one of the top-selling videos in the U.S. in the late nineties, for example. And though anime has long had a strong adult following outside Japan, in the mid-nineties its influence began to reach kids, too, as popular anime series like *Sailor Moon* and *Dragon Ball* began to be re-packaged and re-voiced for the world market. *Sailor Moon* — about a boy-crazy, junk-food-addicted teenage girl who morphs into a superhero to battle evil aliens — became wildly popular with pre-teen girls after its 1996 premiere in Canada. On the other hand, adults, particularly parents of *Sailor Moon* fans, were alternately bewildered and appalled by the show. *Sailor Moon*, created in an anime style typical for Japanese TV, looked to North Americans like nothing so much as a cheesy comic-book-in-motion, with its quick cuts and pulsating visuals. Grown-up befuddlement grew to epic proportions with the rise of the anime craze that ended the millennium — *Pokémon*. (I'll be taking a closer look at this a bit later in the book. For now, suffice it to say that *Pokémon* is the exception that proves the rule: an example of anime with absolutely no adult appeal.)

With anime making its mark on global popular culture, the way is being paved for animation to finally be judged by the same artistic standards as so-called adult art forms. The artist most responsible for the high estimation in which anime is held is unquestionably Hayao Miyazaki, who has been called the Walt Disney of Japan. Miyazaki has helmed his own studio since the early eighties, and his films have enjoyed tremendous popularity in his native country. But only since 1993, with the U.S. release of *My Neighbor Totoro* on video, has his work begun to reach a sizable audience outside of Japan. Miyazaki's films can be a stretch for North American audiences. Certainly Uncle Walt never dreamed up anything as darkly complex as *Princess Mononoke*. Second only to *Titanic* in Japanese box-office sales, the animated feature was praised as a work of genius by many critics. One called it an epic about "no less than the passing of mankind from pagan beliefs into a complex, ruinous modernity." But North American acclaim was accompanied by the belief that it wasn't suitable for children. Most reviewers who praised *Mononoke*, such as Ty Burr in *Entertainment Weekly*, stressed that it was "unquestionably not one for the kiddies" because of its brutal violence and brooding, dark subject matter.

The critics might have been right in the case of *Princess Mononoke*. (Though I admire the film, I found it awfully long, with a dense, convoluted story difficult for a young audience to follow.) Overall, I think kids are hungry for darker and more challenging stories than the usual stuff that's offered to them. When Miyazaki came to the Toronto International Film Festival in 1999, he insisted that he'd made the film for all ages, including children. Admitting that *Mononoke* was a departure from his earlier, sunnier films *My Neighbor Totoro* and *Kiki's Delivery Service*, Miyazaki spoke about his desire to make challenging material for children in terms that, until recently, were almost unheard-of in the world of family films:

> Our goal with those films has been to send a message of hope and
> the possibility of happiness to growing children. But the truth is that
> those children ... are worried about the direction of humankind;
> they're worried about the continuation of the future of the world.
> And what we realized was that by continuing to make movies that
> only taught them about hope and happiness, we were in fact turning
> a deaf ear to their very urgent needs and pleas.[4]

Harry Potter and the Woodstock Moment

The turn of the millennium was marked by a pair of kid crazes, one of which showed that to a certain extent the gap between the generations was alive and well. Adults couldn't make head nor tail of the bizarre characters and arcane lore of *Pokémon* or its equally confounding successor, *Digimon,* and most of them didn't care to try. But the second craze was a stunning example of the blurring of the generational lines, and the blending of children's and adults' tastes. Harry Potter is the boy-wizard and hero of the phenomenally popular books by British writer J.K. Rowling. When *Harry Potter and the Philosopher's Stone* was published in 1997, it was an immediate success, and was soon followed by a pair of sequels (the title for the first book was changed to *Harry Potter and the Sorcerer's Stone* for the U.S. market). But no one could have foreseen that Harry Potter would become a moment of such astonishing pop convergence, as well as a phenomenon without precedent in children's publishing.

Not that previous children's books haven't met with comparable success. By the mid-nineties, New York-based writer R. L.

Stine's "Goosebumps" series of horror novels had sold more than 250-million copies, making him one of the all-time best-selling authors. But "Goosebumps" was strictly for the kids. There were no illusions that these big-print, formulaic horror stories, which Stine managed to churn out at the rate of two a month, would have the slightest appeal for adults. This simply reflects the prevailing wisdom in the publishing industry — adult fiction is for grown-ups, juvenile fiction is for kids, and never the twain shall meet. Juvenile fiction is considered a lower life-form. It also has a built-in invisibility. This is because the few regular venues for reviews of books for children are usually confined to periodicals and papers targeted at teachers and librarians. The luckier authors might get an odd mention in children's books columns in a few of the major newspapers.

The books aren't just ghettoized, though. They're also completely defined by age segregation. There are two broad categories: picture books and chapter books. The first category is for young children, who must be read to and who need strong visual stimulation to keep them interested. Chapter books are narratives that more closely resemble adult novels. They are meant, for the most part, to be read by children themselves. It's within the category of chapter books that the fetish for age categorization is carried to often ridiculous extremes: there are Early Readers, Young Readers, Middle Readers, Young Adults and any number of other terms. This is done for marketing purposes, and has little bearing on what kids actually read or how they choose what to read. It creates an arbitrary, overlapping mishmash, as different retailers label and shelve kids' books according to their own peculiar practices. In a single day, I checked out four different retailers and found my fantasy novel, *The Nordlings*, in four different sections.

The Harry Potter phenomenon successfully defies such age categorization. Even pre-schoolers know all about the books. They've heard about Quidditch and Hogwart's School of Wizardry and they want to get in on the fun. They clamor to have the books read to them, and they're completely undeterred by the lack of pictures. But even more striking is the way grown-ups have taken to the books. For what child-audiences were to the success of *Titanic,* adult readers have been to Harry Potter. The books have shot up adult bestseller lists in every country they've been introduced into. The Canadian publisher of the series, Raincoast Books, put out a separate edition with a more subdued, grown-up cover design to appeal to adult readers. Some bookstores even sold this version at an "adult" price — almost twice as much as the one with the kid-friendly cover. The culmination of Rowling's breakthrough came in the fall of 1999, when the first three books in the series simultaneously occupied the number one, two and three spots on *The New York Times* bestseller list.

That remarkable feat made it abundantly clear that Harry Potter had transcended the kid-lit ghetto, but the fallout from it provided some telling insights into some longstanding assumptions. Sales of children's books have traditionally been tallied separately from sales of adult fiction. When the *Times* broke with this practice, it was simply acknowledging just how big this phenomenon had become. Still, few publications followed the *Times'* lead. *Publishers' Weekly* and most of the big dailies continued to chart the books on a separate children's list, despite the overwhelming evidence that Harry Potter sales were outstripping well-established adult fiction bestsellers by the likes of Stephen King and John Grisham. The Toronto *Globe and Mail* put the series' books on the adult list, but consigned to a Special Interest section with cookbooks and pop psychology. There was even grumbling in some quarters that the *Times'* practice was robbing some writers of their rightful place on the list. One literary agent complained to *Entertainment Weekly,* "For somebody who's been writing adult fiction for a long time to be No. 17, not No. 15, because there are two children's books up there, that's very frustrating and, more than that, career-damaging." (Ah, poor author stuck at number seventeen, I feel your pain, truly I do.) For some literary watchers, the last straw came with the news that the third book in the series, *Harry Potter and the Prisoner of Azkaban,* had come within a hair's breadth of winning the prestigious Whitbread book prize, losing to Nobel prize-winning poet Seamus Heaney's translation of *Beowulf* by a single vote. One churlish critic scolded "readers who refuse to grow up" for having the temerity to suggest "that *Harry Potter* should be treated as a masterpiece for adults" while another pronounced that it would be a "national humiliation" for Britain if *Harry Potter* won the Whitbread.

The Harry Potter juggernaut shows no signs of abating. Much like the scar on Harry's forehead, lightning seems to have struck the series. The anticipation for the fourth book put it at the top of the Amazon.com bestseller list a full six months before its scheduled publication date. And when *Harry Potter and the Goblet of Fire* was finally unleashed on the world in July, 2000 — in a military-style operation shrouded in secrecy — it triggered a frenzy that a spokeperson for Scholastic, the book's American publisher, characterized without a trace of irony as "the single biggest event in the history of bookselling." People camped out in front of stores, and retailers hosted midnight slumber parties right in the stores. As it sold at a furious clip, the superlatives flew thick and fast. A few weeks after *Goblet of Fire* was released, Greg Gatenby, the organizer of Toronto's International Festival of Authors, confidently announced that J.K. Rowling's reading at the city's enormous Skydome in the fall of 2000 would constitute "the biggest literary event in history." (As it turned out, while Gatenby's boast was true in a Guinness-Book-of-Records kind of way, the 50,000 capacity venue was less than half full for the event.)

The release of the fourth *Harry Potter* book was also the first real test of the Internet's ability to deliver the goods, and deliver it did. Saturday, July 8, 2000 was widely hailed as a banner day in the history of e-commerce, with the largest single-day delivery of an online item. The big American retailers Amazon and Barnes & Noble arranged for same-day delivery through private couriers, while in

Canada, the Chapters chain persuaded Canada Post to do the same, even though the federal postal service doesn't normally deliver on Saturdays. Some smaller chains and stores even offered free door-to-door delivery to their favored customers.

The reason for Harry Potter's success was the subject of much media debate. Was it due, as *New York Times* reviewer Janet Maslin enthused, "to the radically simple fact that they're so good"? Or was the phenomenon yet another example of the power of hype? Canada's resident curmudgeon, Rex Murphy, wrote of it this way in his *Globe and Mail* column: "a megadose of fandom and faddishness, a global full-body immersion into numbing conformity and the need to have something now because everyone else who counts is going to have it now." One media expert, Robert Thompson of Syracuse University, chalked up much of the books' appeal to baby-boomer nostalgia for the pre-television and video-game era. Many parents, Thompson told *The Toronto Star,* were embracing Harry Potter for the simple reason that he wasn't in a TV show or a video game, but in a *book:* "We believe the act of reading itself is going to rescue our children from teenage pregnancy and all the ills of modern adolescence. That's the real fantasy here: The nostalgic idea that if we would simply quit watching TV and video games, a rainbow would descend and we'd lock hands and live happily ever after."[5] Even as Thompson made his pronouncement, a Harry Potter video game was in the works — though the software developer, Electronic Arts, was worried that the mania might fade in the year or two it would take to bring the game to market.

There were also fears about a flood of Harry Potter merchandise. The author said that the prospect of Harry figures turning up in Happy Meal boxes was her "worst nightmare" and vowed to do anything to prevent that from happening. But Harry's creator has little control over a pop culture event of this magnitude, and even as Rowling spoke, the great merchandising juggernaut had already been set in motion. Mattel and Hasbro climbed on board to push, among other things, plush toys, action figures, a trivia game, packs of Bertie Bott's Every Flavor Beans (Harry's favorite candy), even Harry-themed bedroom furniture. Warner Bros., producer of the first *Harry Potter* movie, offered not-terribly-convincing reassurances that the company would be protective of the Potter franchise and refrain from flooding the market with product tie-ins. In fact, many licensees were taking a wait-and-see approach, since the branding and merchandising of a book character had never been tried on this scale before. Did kids really want Harry Potter sheet sets on their beds? Or did they just want to read the books?

Speaking of which, let's get back to what was happening between the books' covers. The most fascinating — and largely unremarked-upon — aspect of the series is the royal treatment it received from media outlets. Typically, children's novels don't even register on the cultural radar; only a few receive even minimal notice when they're released. But the *Harry Potter* books have been accorded a level of attention and credibility from adults that no previous children's book has ever been deemed worthy of. When *Goblet of Fire* came out in the summer of 2000, children's writers who had labored in obscurity for years saw this book reviewed by *The New York Times'* Maslin and *Salon* magazine's Charles Taylor — critics who normally devote their attention to capital-L literature. *The Globe and Mail* lined up reviews from no fewer than four adult writers over a two-day span. Though most of the reviews were overwhelmingly positive — Maslin prounounced the book a classic, as did Joan Acocella in *The New Yorker* — there were a few negative voices. Most notable among them was Anthony Holden, one of the Whitbread judges, who dismissed Rowling's entire oeuvre as "Disney cartoons written in words." Regardless, a sentiment voiced frequently in reviews and by the reading public at large was that the Potter series was superior, something set apart from the great mass of ordinary children's books. "They're well written and genuinely funny," said one twenty-five-year-old fan. "That's kind of rare for a kid's book."

Comments like that only betray the public's ignorance of children's and young-adult fiction. Even most of the mainstream reviewers of the Potter books were Johnny-come-latelys to kid-lit. In fact, an oft-expressed sentiment in reviews by more knowledgable writers was that the *Harry Potter* books were well written and well crafted, but — compared to the work of other young-adult fantasy writers — not terribly original. Sean French, the *London Times* critic, for example, mentioned the similarly themed "Worlds of Chrestomanci" series by British writer Diana Wynne Jones, which he judged far superior to Rowling's work. The names of fellow fantasists Susan Cooper, Madeleine L'Engle and Philip Pullman have also cropped up in Potter reviews. None of these authors are slouches in the sales department, and all have received awards and acclaim — Cooper for her "The Dark is Rising" series, L'Engle for the classic *A Wrinkle in Time* and its sequels and, most recently, Pullman for his novels *The Golden Compass* and *The Subtle Knife.* But for all their devoted readers and critical accolades, none has experienced anything remotely like the success of J.K. Rowling.

Personally, I agree that Rowling's real genius is as a synthesizer rather than a breaker of new ground in children's stories. But there's no question about her storyweaving skills. Cumulatively, the books exert a powerful appeal that works almost, for lack of a better word, like a spell. I've seen some fairly jaded kids who felt ho-hum about the first book get slowly but surely drawn into the second. By the third, they're hooked. Not to mention grown-ups, who are drawn to the simple pleasures of the series' narrative. As with the characters of Charles Dickens (and unlike so much contemporary literary fiction) things *happen* with Harry Potter, and the books have made it cool for adults to read stories once again.

In the end, trying to explain a phenomenon like Harry Potter is probably as fruitless as trying to explain why lightning strikes one place rather than another. Canada's Rex Murphy wrote that, with the release of the fourth *Harry Potter* book, "the 7- to 11-year olds have their own Woodstock moment," and though his comment was meant sardonically, there's a sense in which it's perfectly true: this *was* a defining moment, not just for this generation, but for seven- to eleven-year-olds still to come. Because the real driving force behind J.K. Rowling's success is the emergence of a new demographic, economic and cultural force: the powerful Tweens.

NOTES

1. Philippe Ariès, *Centuries of Childhood,* translated from the French by Robert Baldick (New York: Vintage Books, 1962), 50.
2. Ibid., 57.
3. Ibid., 79.
4. Norman Wilner, "No Good and Bad Guys in Princess Mononoke," *The Toronto Star* 2 November 1999, F8.
5. Daphne Gordon, "Nostalgia Feeds Harry Hype," *Toronto Star* 9 July 2000, D10.

MARCH OF THE TWEENS

A WHILE BACK, Ivy informed me that she needed some new underwear. No problem, I told her, figuring I'd pick up one of those three-pair packs of girls' panties somewhere on my travels the next day. No, she said. Not this time.

"I want to pick them out myself. At La Senza Girl."

I was familiar with La Senza, a successful Canadian lingerie and leisure-wear chain. And I'd recently heard that the company was opening some new outlets targeting pre-teen girls. Word of the new store had spread quickly among Ivy's friends. I was curious to check it out myself, so off we went.

From the moment we walked into the store, La Senza Girl screamed fun. The decor was cool chrome dotted with fur-covered telephones and oversized wavy-legged stools. Near the entrance we saw racks of skimpy tank tops and ankle-length spaghetti-strap dresses in hip metallic colors like pearl and mauve. Ivy was very taken with the tank tops, but I ushered her past them until we found what we'd come for: several tables with neatly laid-out rows of girls' underpants. But they weren't like the waist-high, flowery-print ones that I would have bought her at the department store. These were low-slung, hipster bikinis in stripes and geometric prints: underpants that looked pretty much like the kind of underpants I wear.

On an adjoining table were stretchy cotton/spandex sports bras — I noticed they avoided calling them training bras — in the same sizes. While Ivy was picking out her lingerie (shopping at La Senza Girl means you've graduated from underwear to lingerie), I went to look at a nearby rack full of T-shirts and pajamas with adorable round-faced figures on them. I recognized these characters immediately from the "Little Miss" books I used to read to Ivy when she was a toddler. This is a perennially popular British series of simple stories, each one revolving around a character with a single, sometimes charmingly flawed trait. Two- and three-year-old girls just love them. And sure enough, there was a display of the books themselves for sale — *Little Miss Scatterbrain, Little Miss Plump* and — one of Ivy's old favorites — *Little Miss Twins.*

No wonder Ivy and her friends are flocking to shop here, where little-girl memories are combined with big-girl lingerie in a shopping environment designed to help them identify — to borrow the marketers' lingo — "with the demographic they aspire to." It's a sure-fire formula to rope in pre-teen girls, suspended as they are between the bodies they're growing out of and the hormone-besotted teenagers they're becoming.

Early Bloomers?

The 20th century ushered in an unprecedented focus on child development and child rearing: the groundbreaking studies of Jean Piaget, which laid the foundation for modern cognitive development theory; the bonding and maternal separation theories of psychologists D.W. Winnicott and John Bowlby; the voluminous (and still-growing) body of research on the effects of daycare. Altogether, that's a great deal of attention on the stage of life known as early childhood, from birth to roughly age six. Similarly, the coining of the term adolescence by psychologist G. Stanley Hall in the twenties ushered in an era of concern regarding teenagers and what to do about them (a study that borders on being a collective obsession). But traditionally, the in-between kids — the seven- to twelve-year-olds — have gotten short shrift. Sigmund Freud himself called the pre-teen years the latency period, believing that children's sexuality, after being engulfed in the Oedipal struggles of early childhood, flamed out and went underground until the hormonal surge of adolescence brought it back up to the surface.

Look out, world. Pre-teens are latent no more. They're finally getting noticed in a big way by marketers and media-watchers, who've struggled to come up with a label to describe them. (Though no self-respecting kid I know would be caught dead using the term tween, it seems to have taken hold. I'll use it for purposes of convenience here.) No group embodies the contradictions surrounding modern childhood more than these kids do. Nowadays, adults are having an awfully hard time figuring out just what is appropriate for kids who've outgrown Disney but aren't ready for prime time. Today's kids are exposed to sexuality — in dress, imagery and song lyrics — at an age when, in past decades, they were expected to have several more years of sheltered ignorance. The sexualization of the tween years outweighs commercialization as a source of parental anxiety: adults are far more distressed at the prospect of tweens dressing sexily than at the thought of them being molded into model consumers.

Much of this anxiety came to a head in the Spice Girl craze of the late nineties. Magazines were filled with stories like "Is Girl Power too Sexy for Young Girls?" Parents lamented that almost overnight their daughters had switched allegiance from Barney to the Spice Girls. One mother, seeing a group of girls trouping off to a Spice Girls concert, sighed to a reporter, "These are kids. They should be doing kid things." Models as young as fifteen appeared in fashion shows and on magazine covers. One such model, Bijou, made her runway debut at thirteen. And the reigning successor to the Spice Girls, singer Britney Spears, changed in a few short years from a Mouseketeer on the Disney Channel to an object of male Lolita fantasies, with navel-baring outfits and the lyrics "I'm not that innocent." Parental worries weren't confined to girls, what with reports of eleven- and twelve-year-old boys wearing cologne and rating the girls in school.

In a sense, the tween phenomenon can be viewed not so much as a separate demographic group than as a downward expansion of adolescence. Simply put, tweens are today's teenagers, behaving like teens well before they chronologically become them. Adolescence, at least in its cultural sense, is beginning three to five years earlier than it used to. Sometimes more. People my age, who grew up in the fifties and sixties, can see this clearly in pop music. The kind of music that interested me and my friends at age thirteen and fourteen, my daughter and her friends were already immersed in by the age of nine. There's evidence that other time-honored adolescent rites of passage are happening earlier, as studies show that more kids between the ages of ten and thirteen are engaging in the kind of risk-taking behavior traditionally associated with teenagers, such as smoking and shoplifting.

Put another way, there's no longer a clear link between adolescence and the onset of puberty. This means a distinction has to be made between physical and cultural maturation. When we ask questions like "Are kids today growing up too fast?", we need to be more specific about what we mean by growing up. To further complicate matters, there's an ongoing controversy over what exactly constitutes the onset of puberty, and whether it, too, is moving downward. A much-publicized 1997 study of 17,000 girls in the United States found that the average age for breast development and the other physical changes of puberty had moved down to nine, two years younger than what has been considered the norm since the sixties. The head researcher, Dr. Marcia Herman-Giddens, concluded that her data strongly suggested that the trend toward earlier puberty is real. She recommended that puberty classes, which currently start in grade 5 in Canada and the U.S., begin at least two grades earlier. A British study concluded that one in six girls shows signs of puberty by the age of eight, and that half of all girls are now entering puberty by ten.

Different studies suggest a number of possible causes for early puberty. In 2000, some Spanish researchers reported a link between early pubertal development and low birth weight in babies. Others studies point to the use of soy-based infant formulas, which contain substances that mimic the female hormone estrogen. Environmentalists are concerned about indications that pubertal changes are being triggered by children's exposure to growth hormones (in meat and dairy products), pesticides and other contaminants. A study carried out on Puerto Rican girls suggests that phthalates, chemicals widely used in plastics and other consumer goods, may play a role. Some researchers are even seriously exploring the hypothesis that kids' exposure to sexual content in movies and TV could stimulate hormone production and trigger pubertal changes in pre-teens.

But some experts aren't completely persuaded that puberty is occurring significantly earlier than in the past. Dr. Miriam Kaufman, the head of Adolescent Medicine at Toronto's Hospital for Sick Children, points out that the average age of menarche (the onset of menstrual periods) has remained roughly stable for more than thirty years, occurring by the age of twelve or thirteen for most girls. She suggests that doctors in the past would have missed early signs of puberty because they weren't looking for them, and didn't ordinarily examine naked pre–teen girls. Kaufman also says that dietary changes in recent years are making kids bigger (at least in the developed world), possibly bringing with them puberty-like physical changes.

While there's a considerable range of opinion about whether kids are reaching physical maturity sooner, there is one sense, at least, in which kids clearly *are* growing up faster: almost from the moment of birth, they become capital-C consumers.

KAGOY: Growing Older/Spending Younger

Marketers say that kids today are growing up faster than ever before. Some even say that kids between the ages of three and five are more like eight- or nine-year-olds from decades past, in terms of their brand knowledge and influence, as well as play patterns and relationships with toys.

KidScreen, an industry magazine devoted to advertising and promotion, put this statement to a panel of parents in 1999: seventy-five per cent agreed. The publication even coined a term for the phenomenon: KAGOY, for Kids Are Growing Older Younger. Unlike, say, parents of Spice Girls wannabes, people who work in youth marketing don't feel particularly conflicted about this trend. They're willing to take a clear-eyed look at kids as they really are. Even more importantly, these marketers are eager to get a handle on the inner lives and deepest desires of the subjects of their studies. It is the best way to figure out how to sell stuff to them. To paraphrase a Bob Dylan song, parents and other adults may know what kids need, but the youth marketers know what they *want.* In that sense, they're way ahead of the rest of us.

Nowadays even toddlers are a demographic, and their favorite shows, like *Barney* and *Teletubbies*, aren't just TV characters but brands. It's clear that marketers understand that we've entered a new era, one in which parents are no longer the gatekeepers to the larger world. Advertisers seek a direct pipeline to junior consumers, and one of the key ways they're bypassing parents is the Internet. Kids who shop at La Senza Girl, for instance, get notices of sales and special promotions sent directly to their own e-mail addresses. Like other retailers targeting tweens, La Senza Girl understands that most kids spend far more time online than their parents (a trend I'll explore in the next chapter). Another avenue is in-school marketing programs, which are highly contentious in a time of shrinking budgets for public education.

Tweens are the new teens in another way. What's happening with pre-teens is a striking replay of the late forties and fifties, when teenagers were first discovered as a hitherto-untapped market. Marketing experts took note of the fact that middle-class teens constituted an ideal consumer group: they had disposable income, few responsibilities, and a keen interest in new products. They not only had their own money to spend from part-time jobs after schools and on weekends; they also had a great deal of influence on family spending patterns. These teenagers were the ones who kept track of the latest products, urging their parents to buy cars, appliances — whatever was new and upscale.

A key player in the creation of the new teen market was Helen Valentine, the pioneering first editor of *Seventeen* magazine. Not that Valentine had an easy time of it when she first tried to convince advertisers to court the teenage market. She was one of the first to hire market researchers to study teenagers' spending habits, and used the results to persuade advertisers that this new group existed, and that they needed to be marketed to in a particular way. Valentine created a character, Teena, to represent the typical teenager, and used her to spread the word about these young female consumers. "Teena Means Business, Don't Pass Her By!" was the motto of Valentine's campaign. "Teena ... has money of her own to spend ... and what her allowance and pin-money earnings won't buy, her parents can be counted on to supply. For our girl Teena won't take no for an answer when she sees what she wants in Seventeen." [1] Once the huge numbers of post–war baby boomers began to reach adolescence in the late fifties and early sixties, this new teen market became a major economic force. The result was that whole industries catered to the desires of these youthful consumers, producing specialty cosmetics, pop music, blue jeans and other items specifically tailored to their tastes.

This scenario has been revisited throughout the nineties, as tweens emerged as the latest hot demographic. Like middle-class teens in the fifties, a lot of kids in this younger age group have money to spend. And lots of it: $1.5-billion annually in Canada alone, according to a 1999 study. Where do they get it? While some of them are earning money from traditional kids' jobs like babysitting and raking leaves, the bulk of it comes from their families. Some kids not only get heftier allowances now, but they're able — coming from one- and two-child families — to coax considerable amounts out of their parents for the things they want. Like Teena, they "won't take no for an answer." Many also have well-off grandparents who are prepared to spend lavish amounts of money on gifts. An increasing number of kids between the ages of nine and fourteen have bank accounts, with their own personalized bank cards to flash around on the playground. Banks, aware of the importance of establishing early brand-loyalty, are courting tweens, offering them specialized services that are a far cry from the old kiddie starter accounts that used to sit with $25 balances for months on end. Add to this the fact that, unlike grown-ups, tweens don't have rents or mortgages, and unlike many teenagers, they're not carrying car payments. All that money is, as one thirteen-year-old bragged to a *Globe and Mail* reporter, "100 per cent disposable."

While tweens have more money to spend, it's the fact that there are so *many* of them that is the real source of their enormous economic clout. Demographic experts predict that the so-called Echo generation will easily surpass their parents, the baby boomers, in their impact on the economy. And, numbering in the neighborhood of 60 million in North America alone, they far outnumber their Gen-X predecessors by a factor of three. Marketing executive Nat Puccio told *The Wall Street Journal* that the new generation of tweens has the critical mass to "begin challenging the baby boomers for cultural, social and marketplace supremacy." Puccio and other marketing analysts view the rise of the Echo generation as a kind of passing of the torch — the consumer torch, that is — and for the better part of the past decade, retailers have been rubbing their hands in anticipation.

Tweens' impact was already being felt early in the nineties with the explosion in wireless communications. In fact, they've been referred to as the beeper generation for their eager adoption of all the new devices. Pagers and cell phones were embraced first by teens, then pre-teens; both became as much fashion accessories as devices to keep in touch. Wireless companies frankly admitted that they were targeting young consumers, making products in bright colors and featuring kids in their ad campaigns. One communications executive told a *Globe and Mail* reporter, "I see our addressable market as being eleven and above." Perhaps the ultimate sign of the popularity of these gadgets came when schools began to ban cell phones and pagers because they were disrupting the classroom. Part of the boom has, of course, been fueled by parents' security concerns. As one ten-year-old told the same reporter, "I got my cell phone for my birthday last month so my parents can always find me." But communication goes two ways, and one important upshot of the wireless revolution has been the way it feeds pre-teens' desire to be on their own.

Tweens are having a huge impact on other sectors of the economy as well. Time was, for instance, when clothes for kids this age were mostly found at department stores and discount chains. I remember how, when my older daughter, Martha, was around eleven, I used to commiserate with other parents about how hard it was to find anything for kids this age. They're not quite big enough for adult clothes and too big or style conscious for kid sizes. The market began to shift in the late eighties, with the introduction of GAPKids, followed soon after by BabyGAP. These stores got parents used to the idea of paying near-adult prices for clothes that kids would grow out of in less than a year. Though GAP's spare, more grown-up look was a departure from the frilly, old-fashioned children's styles, not everyone liked what they saw. Some observers felt it was just replacing one uniform with another. Initially, GAP was slow off the mark in reaching the tween market. Like other retailers, it took a while to clue in to the fact that pre-teens don't want to shop at the same stores as younger kids. But the company made up the lost ground in 2000, with ad campaigns like the successful TV spots featuring hip-looking tweens in their own rock band. They sing "You Really Got Me," a hit song from the sixties that provided built-in retro appeal for parents.

The nineties saw an explosion in fashion aimed at tweens, mostly spin-offs of established and up-market adult chains that are cool enough. The fashion industry in Canada has gotten into the act with chains like RootsKids, Club Monaco Boys and Girls, Le Chateau Junior Girl, and the aforementioned La Senza Girl. These stores carry clothes as well as cosmetics, jewelry, backpacks and more. Even cosmetics and fragrances aimed at young teens have been brought to market by big labels like Calvin Klein and Tommy Hilfiger.

As in the clothing industry, entertainment moguls were also guilty of ignoring the needs and particular tastes of pre-teens. But that began to change in the late nineties, as Hollywood studios noticed that pre-teens were a huge part of the audience for teen movies, and for many adult films too. Pre–teen kids are a big factor in the success of adult TV shows like *Xena, Warrior Princess* and *Buffy the Vampire Slayer*. Increasingly, kids in this age group account for a large sector of the audiences of cable stations like the Food Network, counting the high-energy cooking shows *Emeril Live* and *Iron Chef* among their favorites. Tweens' impact has been felt even more keenly in the rise of powerful youth networks in the nineties — Nickelodeon in the U.S. and YTV in Canada. These networks offer children's programming that's more sophisticated than the established networks, while less earnest and more clearly commercial than PBS fare. They've become hugely important shapers and reflectors of kids' tastes.

In pop music, tweens were responsible for the success of such major pop phenoms of the late nineties as the Spice Girls, the Backstreet Boys, Britney Spears and 'N Sync. Noting the popularity of summer music fests like Lollapalooza and Lilith Fair among older teens, Nickelodeon launched what it called "the first-ever kids' music festival" in the summer of 1999. Aimed at an audience between ages eight and thirteen, the forty-city tour featured the second-tier acts 98 Degrees and Monica. Concert venues even began providing quiet rooms, complete with free coffee, for parents accompanying their kids to shows. (Taken to a rock concert by mom? Elvis and Jimi Hendrix must be rolling over in their graves.) Tweens aren't just buying music, they're making it: creating a subgenre some industry observers have deemed lunchbox pop. The best known tween-rocker is twelve-year-old Aaron Carter, younger brother of one of the Backstreet Boys. Pre–teen artists are represented in other musical genres as well. Soprano Charlotte Church first created a sensation at the age of twelve with her opera-lite effort *Voice of an Angel*. Country singer Billy Gilman was barely thirteen when his first album was released. Hip-hop has its own tween practitioner in the person of Lil' Bow-Wow — a young protégé of rapper Snoop Dogg.

Tweens are revolutionizing print, too. The past decade has seen a boom in youth-oriented magazines, many of them spin-offs of adult publications. *Teen People* premiered in 1998 and, like its parent, found instant success profiling celebrities. According to *Teen People* editor Christine Ferrera, pre-teen kids are "defining pop culture for the rest of the country." *Cosmopolitan* got into the act with *Cosmogirl*. The premiere issue profiled tween fave Melissa Joan Hart, star of *Sabrina, the Teenage Witch,* and featured back-to-school fashions. Taking a page from Oprah's book, TV's Olsen twins — known to kids since their turn as child stars on *Full House* — brought out a new lifestyle magazine bearing their name in 2000.

Nor is the book world immune to tween power. In the nineties, the eight-to-thirteen market grew into one of the most lucrative areas of publishing. Kids scooped up fanzines and quickie biographies of their favorite stars (*'N Sync: The Official Book, Leonardo DiCaprio: The Unauthorized Biography*) and fantasy novel series like *Animorphs*. Perhaps the ultimate indicator that tweens are making their mark on book culture is that, with the publication of *Chicken Soup for the Preteen Soul* in 2000, they now have their own volume in the phenomenally popular series.

Crazed Collectibles

Though they're moving into traditionally adult territory in some areas, tweens are still kids who like to play. But figuring out *what* they want to play with has proven a challenge for toy manufacturers, who in recent years have been grappling with declining markets due to what's known as age compression. Time was when seven- to eleven-year-olds could be counted on to play with Lego and Barbie dolls. But now these kids are abandoning childhood toys for video and computer games.

The appeal of at least one sector of the toy market remains undiminished for tweens. Accumulating, ordering, naming, trading and assigning value to collectibles are all prime impulses of the pre-teen mind. Particular items go in and out fashion — who'd be caught dead with a stamp collection these days? — but the drive to collect things continues. A decade ago, my daughter Martha and her friends were completely caught up in sticker trading. There were a dizzying variety of styles — fuzzies, smellies, glitter stickers — and they had a system of value too complex to be understood by anyone but a ten-year-old. Compared to some of the more recent collecting crazes, stickers were a parents' dream: blandly cute, small enough to press into an album and, best of all, cheap. Other not-so-cute collectibles that gained popularity around the same time were Troll dolls — with their fuzzy Day-Glo hair and endlessly variable outfits — and Garbage Pail Kid cards, which mocked the Cabbage Patch doll craze with gross humor. Traditionally, kids' collecting interests have been largely determined by gender: boys wouldn't be caught dead with sticker albums; girls were bored to tears by sports cards. But in the mid-nineties, a craze came along that not only crossed the gender divide but brought kids' collecting to a whole new level of intensity. POGS were bottlecap-sized discs of varying value that could be won or lost in fiercely competitive games of toss. It was the first fad to be widely banned from schoolyards and, though the craze burned out fairly quickly, it left in its wake a legacy of increased complexity and commercialization in kids' collecting.

Adults have developed an interest in kids' collectibles, too. Mattel, for instance, has been manufacturing entirely separate lines of high-priced Barbies for grown-ups for the past couple of decades. Adults really got on the collecting bandwagon, though, with Beanie Babies, and their involvement caused the prices of the plush bean-bag creatures to spiral upward. They were hawked on home shopping channels, and the media carried stories about travelers being stopped at the U.S.–Canadian border with carloads of them being smuggled south for resale. Certain Beanie Babies were made in limited runs to drive up their value. Then, finally, the announcement that all Beanie Babies in circulation would be retired at the end of 1999 set off a continental feeding frenzy among young and old fans.

Adults' collecting mania began to affect kids' attitudes toward Beanie Babies, as I saw played out among Ivy and her friends. They loved their cute, cuddly little animals and piled them in great heaps on their beds. But at the same time, the kids explained to me with high seriousness, you should never cut the labels off, because one with a label was worth more money. One time Ivy found a Beanie Baby that had been dropped in the street near our house. She and her friends thought it was valuable, which sparked a spirited debate over whether she should try to locate the owner and return it, or keep it and see how much money she could get for it. She eventually did find the owner and returned it, because it was The Right Thing To Do. (And, as it turned out, this particular Beanie was not nearly as valuable as they thought.) I could see how these kids were torn between want-ing something for itself, and wanting it because it might be worth a lot of money. In a sense, that's the whole impetus behind collecting, especially in its adult version: to own, rather than to use or enjoy. It's the difference between a messy-haired, played-with Barbie and a mint-condition, perfectly coiffed Barbie in the original, never-opened package.

The dilemmas that surfaced with Beanie Babies were exaggerated tenfold with Pokémon cards, though adults weren't in the picture. In fact, to most grown-ups the phenomenon was something akin to a children's cult. Parents and teachers complained that they couldn't make head or tail of Pokémon's complex, arcane fantasy world. But that was the very reason it appealed to kids, with its endless possibilities for ordering, naming and categorizing. Even the "gotta catch 'em all" mantra — which adult critics regarded as nothing more than an unabashed marketing ploy — was just part of the ever-evolving nature of the story line. Nevertheless, the cards sparked a wave of media controversy everywhere they were introduced. Teachers, who had vivid memories of the temporary insanity of POGS a few years earlier, said they'd never seen a craze to rival Pokémania. One of the main factors fuelling the craze was the intrusion of commercial concepts of value into kids' play and trading.

In 1999 a group of parents in New York launched a class-action suit against the makers of the cards, charging that the company was encouraging gambling addiction in kids by creating artificial scarcities. The suit drew criticism as an overreaction to a harmless kids' fad, but the parents did have a point. Trading became very intense, and feelings ran high when valuable cards were at stake. Little kids as young as four and five, eager to get in on the action, got suckered into bad trades by older ones. In fact, one such situation led to a schoolyard stabbing in Montreal, when a boy tried to recover his younger brother's card collection, an incident reminiscent of the earlier *Power Rangers*-era hysteria.

The real problem with Pokémon was that it introduced commercial notions of value into children's play in an unprecedented way. Pokémon has been called the kids' equivalent to bond trading, and when you think about it, there's not that much difference between playing with these cards and playing the stock market. Not long ago, I saw a TV commercial for Wal-Mart that gives a tangible sense of how far these adult notions of value have penetrated into kids' culture. In the ad, a woman shows off her collection of toys, numbering in the hundreds — Hot Wheels, Barbies and TransFormers, all purchased at Wal-Mart — which she's keeping in the original, unopened boxes. She explains, without a trace of irony, that the collection is for her children — not to play with now, but as a legacy for when they grow up, when the toys will presumably be worth good money to collectors.

The iron law of collecting crazes, however, is that they eventually peter out. Even Pokémon-card addiction didn't prove to be permanent. Another truism is that, by the time the media first get wind of a craze, it's already peaked in the kid world. And by the time blanket media coverage kicks in, the kids have already moved on. When *Harry Potter* author, J.K. Rowling, came to Toronto last year, I was contacted by a Canadian network show. It wanted kids for an in-studio audience while Rowling was interviewed. I called around to several of the pre-teens I knew who were fans of the books, and was surprised at the general lack of interest. "I might have a couple of months ago," one jaded kid told me, "but not now." Another turned me down saying, "J.K. Rowling is just a *normal* person." (I could see her point, actually. In her mind, Harry Potter was the star. She would've gone to see Harry, but not his creator.) The last word on the subject was delivered to me by Ivy herself, in a sort of Pop Culture 101 mini-lecture. "Mom," she sighed, "it's not a kid thing anymore. It's a media thing."

Kidfluence Peddling

Helen Valentine's insight that teenagers were exerting a major influence over their parents' purchases as well as their own turned out to be her most persuasive argument in wooing advertisers to *Seventeen*. It's another fifties pattern being reproduced in the nineties, except this time advertisers don't need to be convinced that tweens are playing a crucial role in deciding how the family money is spent. They've come up with a term — kidfluence — to describe the increasing sway that children hold over family buying patterns. Tweens regularly play the role of information gatherer on a wide range of products; from clothes, telling their parents which labels are hot, to health foods, about which many nutrition-conscious kids are more knowledgeable than grown-ups. According to market analysts, children in the U.S. directly influenced $146-billion in spending on food and beverages alone in 1999. And with their greater technological savvy and knowledge of pop culture, kids in families with disposable incomes also have a big say in buying high-tech items and other major family purchases. Kidfluence is a major reason we're seeing such a ubiquitous use of children in advertising.

Advertisers are also quick to capitalize on kids' interest in certain products. When the updated VW Beetle came on the market in the mid-nineties, North American tweens invented their own contemporary version of I Spy. It involved scoring points by tapping somebody on the arm and saying "Punch Buggy, no punch backs!" when you spied one. (In some versions of the game, you won extra points for spying a vintage Beetle.) When the game eventually turned up in a TV ad for Pepsi, it was clear that Punch Buggy had run its course, at least as far as kids were concerned. The ultimate in cross-promotion occurred in 2000, when Mattel had Barbie trade in her beloved convertible sedan for a hot-pink VW Beetle.

An even more subtle use of kidfluence was at work in the ad campaign for Apple Computer's iMac. In fact, it's likely that tweens were largely responsible for bringing Apple back from the brink of economic oblivion. For years, the company's products had been losing ground to computers using Windows, the Microsoft operating system. By the mid-nineties, the once-powerful innovator's market share had been whittled down to a paltry 5 per cent, and many industry watchers were predicting the company's demise. Then, in the fall of 1998, Apple introduced the iMac, first in translucent blue-green, and a few months later in glossy colors like tangerine, lime-green and purple. The ads, with a ring of iMacs swirling to the strains of the Rolling Stones' classic "She's like a Rainbow," grabbed kids instantly. The campaign tapped directly into tweens' passion for collectibles. Kids knew perfectly well they couldn't have them all — but the idea of owning one was irresistible for those who could afford it. In households all across North America (including ours), kids were begging parents for a hot new computer. I have to admit I was surprised at the extent to which Ivy got caught up in iMac-mania. Media savvy and often savagely critical of advertising stratagems, she nevertheless went into ecstasy every time the commercial came on. She lobbied mightily for us to buy one, despite our protests that we already had a perfectly good (though pathetically un-hip) household computer.

Other high-tech companies have been just as quick to trade on tweens' technological savvy in their marketing. Ads for wireless phones and long-distance savings plans feature kids in the demographically golden eight-to-fourteen age bracket. As cable companies began to move into high-speed Internet access in the late nineties, they followed suit. In Canada, when Rogers Cable mounted an ad campaign for its Internet access service, it knew just who to pitch to. One ad featured a kid showing a telephone jack to a friend, saying, "Can you believe it? My dad says *this* is how they used to get the Internet." "No way!" the friend retorts. Another features a boy who likens getting the Internet through a phone line to "trying to drink a milkshake through a skinny little straw." An authoritative voice then exhorts parents to get cable access and "give your kid a bigger straw."

But while kids may have an unprecedented influence on their parents' buying habits, marketers know it's still parents who control the purse strings. Some merchandisers, realizing that tweens were big fans of the notoriously profanity-laden *South Park,* were careful to tone down the slogans on T-shirts and other paraphernalia to avoid incurring parents' wrath, and to make the shirts acceptable to the bigger family-friendly chains. It is parents' upscale aspirations that are causing a boom for everything from designer children's bedroom furniture to computer camps to fast-track tutoring services.

Valentine's other key insight in shaping the *Seventeen* of the fifties — that companies selling to teenagers had to adopt new marketing strategies, tailor-made to their interests and tastes — is one that holds even more true for tweens. By the time kids reach the preteen years, a good part of marketers' work is already done for them. From riding in supermarket carts as babies to years of watching Saturday morning TV, these are kids who've acquired a level of brand-awareness that far surpasses previous generations. A large part of this label-awareness finds its roots in character marketing, a phenomenon explored in exhaustive detail by sociologist Stephen Kline in his 1993 book, *Out of the Garden.* Kline documents how toy marketers establish this brand-awareness, not just through aggressive advertising, but by nurturing kids' identification with the characters and narratives in TV shows. The current crop of tweens has quite literally grown up with these familiar brands — from Sailor Moon to Power Rangers to Pokémon.

Not that character marketing is new; it's been going on for the better part of the last thirty years. But it's grown so much in sophistication and sheer volume that resistance is all but futile. Consider the sobering example of children's author Dr. Seuss, whose real name was Theodor Geisel. During his lifetime, Geisel strongly opposed commercialization of his beloved creations. But after his death in

1991, his widow, Audrey Geisel, opened the floodgates and began to sell licensing rights to a slew of Dr. Seuss characters. With the blockbuster success of the movie *How the Grinch Stole Christmas* (starring Jim Carrey) over Christmas 2000, the Seussification of commercial pop culture was pretty well complete.

Increasingly, marketers are working to establish label-awareness as early as possible, on the assumption that, like imprinting in baby animals, it leads to lifelong brand loyalty: hence BabyGAP translates into GAPKids into adult GAP. Even when kids outgrow certain brands — Huggies pull-up diapers, say — brand loyalty sticks. When children grow up to be parents themselves, the thinking goes, they'll naturally turn to the names and products that are familiar from their childhood. In recent years, companies have made ever more aggressive efforts to get in on the ground floor by establishing in-school partnerships. In the fall of 1999, for example, Wal-Mart announced it would be providing free merchandise to 120 schools the company had "adopted" across Canada. When critics objected, Wal-Mart officials insisted that they weren't after free advertising and that the merchandise came with no strings attached. But the PR value of these kinds of partnerships is all too obvious: kids in the "adopted" schools heard grateful staff acknowledge Wal-Mart's generosity, and saw the company's donation featured as a news item in the media.

Advertisers understand, too, that very young children don't distinguish between ads and programs on TV: to them, it's all entertainment. Even older kids are likely to say, "Stop, I love that ad!" when you're trying to fast-forward through the commercials that interrupt a program you've videotaped. Hence the proliferation of ad techniques that appeal to kids, like shape-shifting characters and high-tech animation. Another tactic that works with tweens is appealing to their drive for independence and autonomy, like YTV's slogan "You Rule!" Earlier in this chapter, I discussed the recent success of junior clothing chains. Their main strategy is to encourage tweens to identify with people older (and hipper) than they are. For that reason, too, product placement has become commonplace in TV shows popular with teens and tweens. The producers of *Dawson's Creek,* for instance, signed a deal with American Eagle Outfitters to provide clothes for the show. Some jeans manufacturers and soft drink companies try to acquire cachet with kids through corporate sponsorship of snowboarding and other sports events. (This approach has its pitfalls, however, since the more a product appeals to pre-teens, the less teens will want to touch it.)

There's also what could be termed the "between-two-worlds" factor in marketing to tweens: hand in hand with their desire to identify up is tweens' eagerness to distance themselves from the things of early childhood. The makers of Crayola crayons, for instance, confronted this problem and developed a solution that's in many ways a textbook case of successful tween marketing. Like many sectors of the toy industry, Crayola discovered in the nineties that they were losing market share, that kids were abandoning crayons earlier than they used to. In 1997, the company launched a new line of colored pencils, Crayola IQ, aimed at pre-teen kids. Instead of the trademark Crayola orange-and-green packaging, Crayola IQ had a redesigned, all-green package that highlighted the product's useful-ness for making maps, graphs and charts at school. By establishing that all-important grown-up identification (while still trading on kids' familiarity with the product), the company managed to avoid the taint of association with little-kids'-stuff, and Crayola IQ became a big hit.

It's a tricky business, this marketing to tweens. Not only are their tastes as fickle and their trends as ephemeral as teenagers', but pre-teens are torn between conflicting desires and pressures. They want to be independent, but the influence of their parents still holds sway. They want to be big, but they're still very close to being little. So it's not surprising that a whole market research industry has grown up to help advertisers figure out how to reach this group. Nickelodeon has been at the forefront of the youth-marketing trend, conducting extensive research and paying kids as young as eight years old to participate in focus groups. The network has been criticized for going into schools to recruit focus groups, and even conducting in-school interviews. Canada's YTV also recruits kids through the public schools for its regular advisory panels known as SWAT (Stay Weird All the Time) teams. It pays participants $40 a session. Some sample questions from their recruiting survey: "If you could be transformed into any character on a YTV show, who would you choose to be?" "Name three material things that kids your age really want to own." "What is a really trendy thing to do on a Saturday afternoon?" Nickelodeon and YTV have a great deal invested in maintaining their reputations of being on the pulse of the hippest, most media-savvy tweens. As Nickelodeon president, Herb Scannell, told an Associated Press reporter in 1999, market research is important because it enables the network to "look at the world from a kid's point of view" and deliver the kind of programming kids want. But it just as clearly enables them to deliver the demographic to their advertisers. Consumer activists have been critical of this increasing intensification in the area of children's marketing. In 2000, a group called on the American Psychological Association to bar its members from working as consultants and market researchers for companies that sell to kids.

Everybody, it seems, wants a piece of tweens. Marketers want to sell to them. Parents want to control them. Many others are ready to write them off as label-obsessed slaves to consumerism. But it's possible that by making tweens the most marketed-to generation in history, companies may be sowing the seeds of their own destruction. Kids are indisputably consumers, but they're also getting better at seeing through the marketing. Companies are all too aware of this fact, which is why each new product, each new ad campaign, is such a frantic race to reach the kids before a sense of "been there, done that" sets in. Even their desire to be seen as individuals who *don't* slavishly follow trends has become corporate fodder, pitched back to them, as one respondent to a *Toronto Star* youth survey caustically put it, as "conformity wrapped in the guise of self-expression ... Instead of 'be young, have fun, drink Pepsi' why don't [they] say it in plain English: 'You're stupid! Give us all your money!'"

This generation may end up surprising us all. With their knowledge of sexuality and their newfound economic clout, it's clear that many tweens have marched out from behind the walled garden of childhood and good luck to anyone foolish enough to try and push them back in. But there's one corner of the modern world where the wall can truly be said to have never existed at all: cyberspace, the frontier where perhaps the most profound revolution in the relationship between adults and children is happening.

NOTES

1. Grace Palladino, *Teenagers: An American History* (New York: Basic Books, 1996), 104.

BRAVE NEW HUMANS

"... regressive for young children ..."
"... symptomatic of the dumbing-down of television ..."
"... vaguely sinister ..."
"... the most market-oriented children's program concept
I have ever seen ..."

THIS IS A SAMPLING OF SOME of the comments made by speakers at a 1998 international symposium on children's television held in London, England. What was this terrible new scourge? An ultra-gentle show for pre-schoolers, set in a land presided over by a smiling sun-baby and populated by four roly-poly, neon-bright creatures who spoke baby babble and desired nothing more than to give and receive big hugs.

Teletubbies has become so familiar that it's hard to remember what a hornet's-nest it stirred up back then. The show, which originated in Britain a year before the symposium, caused a sensation among preschoolers. Merchandise festooned with the big-eyed, smiling faces of Tinky-Winky, La-La, Dipsy and Po was snapped up off the shelves. But on the eve of its North American premiere, opinions were sharply divided at the London summit, where hundreds of industry heavy-hitters had gathered. Some delegates praised *Teletubbies* as innovative and groundbreaking, while others denounced the show as having no educational value for children. *"Teletubbies* features alien-looking babies in an alien-looking world speaking baby talk," Ada Haug, a children's TV executive from Norway, told the conference. "I get this creepy feeling it's very good for making lots of money." The controversy over *Teletubbies* went beyond concerns about commercialism or baby-talk. Words like "creepy" and "bizarre" kept popping up when people tried to describe it; the show seemed to stir some to an almost irrational level of outrage.

There's no denying that *Teletubbies* is a departure from what we've come to expect a children's program to be. Teletubbyland isn't a recognizable neighborhood like *Sesame Street.* Instead, the centerpiece is a Tubbytronic Superdome surrounded by a landscape dotted with strange devices that periodically pop out of the ground to issue directives from disembodied (albeit friendly sounding) voices. And the Teletubbies themselves, with antennae coming out of their heads and television screens implanted in their bellies, really are reminiscent of pop-culture depictions of aliens.

Indeed, they look like nothing so much as machines. Even their creator, British TV producer Anne Wood, calls them technological babies. Readily admitting that *Teletubbies* depicts an environment awash in high-tech devices, Wood explained to delegates at the London symposium that her team at Ragdoll Productions set out to create something that honestly reflected the present lives of kids:

> They're actually living in a world that is in the midst of a technological revolution, and I became fascinated by the fact that these children of two or three now ... will live in a world when they're twenty-three or four that will be quite unrecognizable to us now. So ... we tried to make the world they inhabited a technological world.[1]

To most adults, this is a profoundly discomfiting idea. I think the response to *Teletubbies* has to do with deeper fears about what's happening to childhood and concern that the show violates (or seems to violate) some of our most cherished notions. There's a widespread belief that children are supposed to grow up in Edwardian nurseries clutching teddy bears, not creatures that resemble chubby space aliens. Their stories are supposed to be set in a once-upon-a-time fairy tale backdrop, not in some futuristic dome. *Teletubbies* is more like something out of *Brave New World* than Mother Goose. (Indeed, one critic described it to *Entertainment Weekly* as "the type of show that George Orwell would have come up with if a network had given him a contract to create a children's series ... *1984* meets *The Smurfs*.")

No wonder the show gives so many people the creeps: it embodies some of our worst fears about modernism, the machine age and new technology. The feeling that machines might rob us of our humanity — indeed, that human beings are in danger of *becoming* machines — has been a cultural preoccupation since the late 19th century, finding expression in stories as disparate as Mary Shelley's *Frankenstein* and L. Frank Baum's *The Wizard of Oz*. The Oz books are filled with a fascinating array of half-man, half-machine characters like the Wheelers (who have wheels in place of hands and feet), Tik-Tok the wind-up mechanical man and, best-known of all, the Tin Woodsman, who, in an eerie prefiguring of current medical technology, keeps acquiring new metallic body parts as he loses his limbs in a series of catastrophes.

But the peculiar genius of *Teletubbies* comes from its creators' understanding that children don't share our fear of the new. Objects that look alien and futuristic to us look normal and familiar to them. For example, the voice trumpets that pop out of the ground in *Teletubbies* have been interpreted by some adults as being weirdly fascistic Big Brother devices. But as Wood pointed out at the London symposium, "children are surrounded by disembodied voices, whether it's the baby alarm or other sorts of machinery. So they're not surprised if a voice is heard in the land." Kids are more comfortable with new technology than adults are, simply because they grow up with it. They have none of the same fears to overcome.

In the nineties, some people raised the possibility that this shift might not be so scary. Instead, these cyber-enthusiasts saw something good emerging in our midst as a result of children's interaction with technology. Author Jon Katz lauds children as "citizens of a new order" and the "founders of the Digital Nation" in his 1997 book, *Virtuous Reality.* According to Katz, "Children are at the epicenter of the information revolution, ground zero of the digital world. They helped build it, and they understand it as well or better than anyone."[2] Another writer, Douglas Rushkoff, has coined the term "screen-agers" for contemporary young people. In his book, *Playing the Future,* Rushkoff argues that kids are our evolutionary future, able to adapt to constant change and the cultural turbulence that new technologies bring. Massachusetts Institute of Technology sociologist Sherry Turkle — whose extensive studies of computer users have caused her to become known as the Margaret Mead of cyberspace — concludes that children are carving out new forms of identity, in essence new ways of being human, via their virtual online experiences. Whatever the average technophobe might make of these views, one thing is abundantly clear: kids are far more at home with technology than their elders.

TechnoBabies and CyberKids

Mobile video system (MVS): it's really just a fancy term for a pricey add-on to a new minivan or sports utility vehicle. But sales reps in car dealerships across North America report that sales of MVSs are mushrooming, largely because of kids pressuring their parents to get one. A TV in the car — what could be more emblematic of the technological environment children are growing up in? Still, MVSs have drawn criticism from psychologists and parenting experts, who worry that kids are becoming accustomed to relating to a screen rather than to real live people.

What's happening in the car pales next to the boom in computers, however. Between 1995 and 1999, household use of the Internet jumped more than 400 per cent, mostly thanks to teens and pre-teens — members of the huge demographic bulge dubbed the Echo generation. These same kids are driving the burgeoning software market. Parents, fuelled by the conviction that computer skills are essential, have enrolled children in computer camps when they were as young as four and five. Large numbers of this upcoming generation write and draw for the first time using keyboards and computer screens instead of pencils and paper.

Cradle-to-grave computer use is becoming a reality for a growing part of the population, as evidenced by the booming sales in software and games for preschoolers. There's even a growing market for what's called lapware — computer software aimed at children under the age of two. The pioneer in this field is JumpStart Baby. There's no question that it is baby-friendly: the animation is eye-catching and gently paced, while the easy, press-any-key responsiveness ensures that pretty much anything the child does — even banging all over the keyboard — will yield the same result. (JumpStart Baby even comes with a warning to parents about keeping drool off the keyboard.)

But many child development experts are appalled at the very thought of lapware, arguing that babies need real-world stimulation, not computer simulation. "The immature human brain neither needs nor profits from attempts to 'jump-start' it," psychologist Jane Healy writes in her book, *Failure to Connect: How Computers Affect Our Children's Minds*. "Simply selecting and watching a screen is a pallid substitute for real mental activity." Even some computer enthusiasts are critical of the trend. Jean Armour Polly, author of an Internet source book for families, opines:

> Little kids should be down on the floor banging on pots and spoons, not banging on the keyboard. I saw a Website where you can drag a pine cone over to a sink to see if it floats. Why not just turn off the computer, go outside and pick up a pine cone so the toddler can learn what a pine cone is? [3]

A new host of problems arising from early-childhood computer use is also coming to the fore. Repetitive strain injuries (RSIs) like finger numbness, back pain and eyestrain are being reported in users as young as seven years old, and some researchers worry that what we're seeing now is just the tip of the iceberg.

It isn't just kid-appeal that's driving the children's high-tech market. Today, a lot of parents believe they have to do whatever's necessary to give their kids a head start. The marketing materials for interactive toys and baby software prey on these parental anxieties, with claims like "scientifically proven to stimulate your infant's developing mind." It's all part of a related controversy over the role of computers in education — a complex issue that's beyond the scope of this book. The rush to get technology into schools has drawn harsh criticism from self-described "computer contrarian" author Clifford Stoll, who argues in his book, *High-Tech Heretic,* that computers are lousy tools for teaching kids how to think — and that their role in education has been vastly over-hyped. Stoll's views have been echoed by Alison Armstrong, author of *The Child and the Machine: Why Computers May Put Our Children's Education at Risk.* But others argue that having computers in schools is one important way to bridge the growing digital divide between poor kids and those who grow up in middle-class homes with PCs and Internet access.

Sitting down in front of a monitor is one thing, but computer chips have also been invading kids' toys for some time. These include dolls and plush animals with voice chips, infrared sensors and robotics technology that make them more life-like. Not that this is anything new: since the invention of the alkaline battery, children have been clamoring for toys that "do things." But the new generation of interactive toys has a level of technological sophistication that's light-years beyond Betsey Wetsey and Chatty Cathy. As an executive for the Toys R Us chain rather ominously enthused to *The Toronto Star,* kids nowadays "can think of a toy as coming alive."

One of the first of the new breed was the furry, bug-eyed Furby, which caused a brief sensation (and the predictable Christmas-season shortages) in 1998. Around the same time, My Interactive Barney —

a talking version of the enduringly popular children's TV icon — hit the market, followed a couple of seasons later by the even more sophisticated eSpecially My Barney, which could be hooked up to a special Website. The Christmas season of 2000 brought a veritable flood of high-tech toys, including robotic pets (Poo-Chi, Tekno Puppy), dolls with learning chips ("Amazing Alli — she remembers your name!") and the animatronic My Real Baby, touted by its manufacturer, Hasbro, as the most life-like doll ever created.

The hyper-real quality of some of these toys can be more than a little unsettling. Not long ago, I felt a shiver go up my spine as I watched an ad for Amazing Babies, twin dolls who speak not only to their little-girl owners but to *each other.* But what spooks adults doesn't bother kids. They see TV ads and covet the expensive high-tech toys — which creates problems for parents who can't afford them. And cost isn't the only downside: the jury is still out on the impact that interactive toys are having on children's development. Specifically, there are concerns about how much scope for imaginative play they really offer. If the toy does pretty much everything on its own, how much interacting does the child get to do? One thing that's certain is that these toys are helping to create young people who have a whole new level of comfort and familiarity with technology. Futuristic nightmare scenarios about robots taking over the world may one day seem like little more than quaint fables from a naive, pre–tech era.

This immersion in digital technology continues as children get older and graduate to more grown-up (though equally pricey) playthings. Kids have embraced the new generation of brightly colored mini-computers modelled from the Palm Pilot and other executive organizers. Although earlier hand-held computers like GameBoy had more appeal for boys, girls have been the most eager consumers of the new messaging devices. The Laser Chat, for example, was specifically marketed to them, and iSpy inserts tiny transmitters and receivers in necklaces and other jewelry pieces. With these mini-computers, users can keep track of addresses and phone numbers, play games, go on the Net and trade instant messages. Think of this latter option as the latest version of passing notes in class. Soon after these devices came on the market, teachers began to complain that students were using them to cheat on exams, and many schools have banned their use.

But there's no rolling back the trend, as high-tech devices become fashion statements and keeping in touch is increasingly viewed as a social imperative. Kids who can afford them quickly grow accustomed to the constant availability that cell phones and instant messaging devices offer, to the point where they can't imagine life without them (just as they can only dimly recall the days when telephones had to be plugged into the wall). The devices have become a part of youth subculture, as new ways of using them are created on the fly. One striking example is kids' invention of pager-speak, where they use abbreviations, numbers and visual icons as a kind of shorthand. It was originally developed by pager and chat-room users, with some terms (e.g. 420 to refer to pot) from police radio codes. But the form keeps evolving with the burgeoning popularity of instant messaging. As a kind of secret language, pager-speak has obvious appeal for kids, not least because it's one of the few things in our age-blended culture that their parents haven't got a clue about.

It's All In The Games

Let the adults fuss over whether computers have educational value or not. What kids really want to do is *play* with them. Games are the real reason kids are so completely at ease with the technology. Playing on computers may be the main thing that separates this generation from its elders. It's a latter-day version of the Generation Gap. Put people my age in front of a Nintendo and they will likely be utterly helpless. (I tried GameBoy — once — and I was dead barely after the game started.) Another version of the same syndrome occurred during the Tamagotchi craze of the late nineties. These were the little cyber-pets that had to be virtually fed, put to bed and played with — or else. Parents faced with the responsibility of keeping Tamagotchis alive while their kids were off at school or summer camp suffered a collective anxiety attack.

Growing up playing computer games may be setting some kids apart in even more fundamental ways; there's evidence it may even be changing the way their brains work. Recent studies suggest that some video games simulate a high with each "hit," causing alterations in brain chemistry that are similar to physical addiction. These studies also indicate that kids who are heavy users have higher rates of depression and social isolation. Doom, Mortal Kombat and other blood-and-guts combat games have come under increasing attack since the 1999 shootings at a Littleton, Colorado high school. Critics say there is a major difference between TV violence, in which kids are just passive viewers, and ever more realistic video games, in which they're actively complicit. Some go so far as David Grossman, the former military psychologist I referred to earlier in this book, who subscribes to the view that kids are learning how to kill from playing video games.

There are alternatives to the mastery model typical of combat and sports games. Sherry Turkle points to Tamagotchis and other virtual pets as examples of games based on what she calls the nurturing model, in which the player gets rewarded for taking care of cyber-creatures rather than dominating or killing them off. Despite many adults' impression of Pokémon as just another slice-and-dice combat game, it's an interesting example of something that straddles both models. Though it involves an ample amount of combat, the point of the game is not to kill opponents but to subdue and add them to the player's stable of pokemon (pocket-monsters), which she or he is then responsible for taking care of and training. As one articulate eleven-year-old wrote to *The Toronto Star* during the height of the controversy, the most important aspect of *Pokémon* is the bonds that develop between the pocket-monsters and their trainers: "The show teaches that love and friendship are more powerful than bossing around."

Another widespread belief is that computer games have spawned a generation of kids who have the attention span of a gnat. But in his book, *Playing the Future,* Douglas Rushkoff offers a more positive take on what he calls "postmodern kids" who can multi-task with ease. Rushkoff believes that the surfing mentality so prevalent now started with the TV remote, and sees it as a new, emerging form of "discontinuous intelligence" — holistic, playful and interactive, rather than rigid and linear. This generation, Rushkoff writes, has grown up viewing a fragmented style of narrative as the norm, and he predicts that linear storytelling itself will become obsolete. Whether or not history bears out Rushkoff's prediction, there's no doubt we're witnessing the emergence of a whole different approach to storytelling. The appeal of popular games like Myst and SimCity arises from their fluid narratives, full of multiple, open-ended story lines and ever-evolving universes, an approach that also characterizes the complex fantasy world of Pokémon and other anime-style games. The next wave of virtual-reality entertainment is even more interactive, with story lines in which players follow multiple scenarios and pick their own endings.

In Sherry Turkle's book, *Life on the Screen: Identity in the Age of the Internet,* she makes a compelling case that this generation's ease with computers is giving them a whole new level of comfort with the idea of change. Turkle borrows the notion of *bricolage* from anthropologist Claude Levi-Strauss to characterize the tinkering approach kids instinctively adopt to new technologies. Instead of reading the rule book or manual, as older people tend to do, kids figure things out by *doing*: "This generation of kids," Turkle told *Scientific American* in 1998, "[when they are] confronting digital objects and virtual space, are completely comfortable with — call it cycling through, call it *bricolage,* call it tinkering ... Call it what you wish but it is an acceptance of fluidity that is striking."[4]

Of course, what Turkle is describing here is precisely the quality that drives linear-thinking adults crazy, and frustrates beleaguered parents who are trying to teach their kids the value of finishing what they've started. But this discontinuous intelligence may have even broader implications than anticipated, ones that will give pause to critics of the couch-potato generation. There are indications that playing computer games and even watching TV might make kids smarter. According to Cornell University psychology professor Ulric Neisser, there has been a well-documented rise in children's IQ scores over the past few decades, most markedly in the areas of creative thinking and problem-solving skills. In a January 2001 interview with the Toronto *Globe and Mail,* Neisser said that many researchers attribute this rise to an increase in kids' "visual literacy" fostered by their familiarity with TV and computers.

Clearly, digital technology is transforming the experience of childhood — but not for everyone. The so-called digital divide is real: many families still can't afford a home computer, and large numbers of kids have only limited access to them at school and in libraries. And there are still plenty of kids for whom cyberspace isn't the be-all and end-all, who'd just as soon play a musical instrument or throw a ball around as wield a joystick. Though you might not know it, to look at some of the breathless media reports about young e-business entrepreneurs.

Who Wants To Be A (Teenage) Millionaire?

In 1996, fifteen-year-old Michael Hayman was trying to work out some technical problems on his Website, MyDesktop.com. He sought help from a fellow computer geek he'd met online, thirteen-year-old Michael Furdyk. They became friends and colleagues; that they lived half a planet apart — Hayman in Brisbane, Australia and Furdyk in Toronto, Canada — meant next to nothing to them. They decided to pool their resources to build MyDesktop.com into a successful Internet magazine for computer users. As the business grew, their high-school studies increasingly took a back seat. In 1998, they brought in a new partner, Albert Lai, a university student who was already a successful entrepreneur himself. With Lai's business acumen and Hayman and Furdyk's computer skills, MyDesktop.com was drawing more than 5 million hits a month by mid-1999, allowing the partners to draw hefty salaries and buy a building in suburban Toronto to house the business. In May of that year, MyDesktop.com was bought by Connecticut Internet pioneer Alan Meckler for an undisclosed seven-figure amount. Lai had just turned twenty, Hayman was eighteen, and Furdyk still hadn't finished high school.

Who wants to be a millionaire? To read the news accounts about various dot-com enterprises, you might conclude that the best qualification is being a computer geek under the age of twenty. And it's certainly true that, in the past decade, a rash of successful Net-based enterprises have been started by teenagers. Eighteen-year-old Shawn Fanning created the controversial and revolutionary Web music-sharing site Napster in 1998. Peter and Mark Lampert spend ten to fifteen hours a week on their own music-sharing site, music4free.com. At the ripe old age of eleven, elementary student Keith Peiris started a highly successful Website design business from his home in London, Ontario. (In 1999, the organizers of a major industry software conference initially didn't let Peiris attend, saying he was too young.) And though the majority of these "teen-trepreneurs" are male, some girls are getting in on the action. California high school student Ashley Power, for example, employs thirty people at Goosehead, her influential Website for teenagers.

It's not just teenagers running their own businesses who are having an impact. A phenomenon called downward mentoring is transforming the corporate culture of large companies, as older executives are tutored by employees young enough, in some cases, to be their grandchildren. The traditional corporate ladder and cycle of working life — in which the young are supposed to struggle and make sacrifices in order to achieve power and financial comfort in middle age — is being upended. Instead, a few lucky kids who are too young to vote and barely old enough to drive are making the kind of money their parents' generation worked a lifetime to acquire. And for all the hype about them, teenage Net millionaires are a small part of the new wave of economic opportunities for youth in cyberspace. Kids as young as nine and ten are working as testers for computer game makers, getting paid in real money, not just free games. And up until the dot-com downturn in 2001, plenty of garden-variety computer geeks were making big bucks designing Websites and serving as consultants to new-media companies.

It's become a contemporary cliché that kids are the ones who know how to program the family VCR, that kids have to teach parents how to set up the new computer system and show them how to navigate the Internet. In the past, adults had more knowledge about almost every domain of life than children, but now the tables have been turned. As Don Tapscott, author of *Growing Up Digital,* puts it, with the explosion in new media and the rise of the Internet, "the knowledge hierarchy has been flipped on its head." Kids aren't dependent on adults to learn high-tech skills — *they're* the experts. Tapscott spoke to one parent who echoes the sentiment of many when she says of her twelve-year-old son: "He's leaps and bounds ahead of me, technologically speaking."

Tapscott, for one, thinks this shift is having positive effects on society at large, encouraging adults to treat young people with more respect, and fostering the development of what he calls more open, consensual families. But most adults aren't so sure. They're unnerved by the strange reversal of roles — as if parents had to go to their kids to learn how to drive the family car. In the realm of new technology, the whole notion of age is being turned topsy-turvy. For the first time, the idea that adults should learn from children rather than vice versa is being seriously promoted.

The corporate world's rush to get behind the trend fuelled a wave of new enterprises known as Net incubators. These are companies that provide startup funds and administrative support to techno-savvy young people who want to create their own Web businesses. The head of one such incubator, Matthew Saunders of Toronto-based NRG Group, says companies like his can provide young would-be entrepreneurs with the business experience and acumen that will help them survive beyond start-up. But the fact is that despite the much-hyped success stories like MyDesktop.com, the virtual woods are full of failed e-business ventures begun, in many cases, by kids who would probably have been better off staying in school. One twenty-year-old — who, with partners, had spent more than six months and $200,000 of NRG investment funds trying to launch a Web business — told a reporter for *The Toronto Star,* "We didn't start with an idea, we just knew we wanted to do something on the Internet to make a lot of money."

And what the young can give with their computer expertise, the young can also take away. Much as they've been hailed as the architects and co-creators of the online world, teenagers are just as often portrayed in the media as hackers, vandals and would-be destroyers of the new Web economy. The sensational attacks that shut down Yahoo!, Amazon and other leading Websites last year eventually led to the arrest of a fifteen-year-old Montreal youth going by the online moniker Mafiaboy. The youth, whose identity could not be revealed under Canada's Young Offenders Act, pleaded guilty to charges of mischief and illegal use of a computer. Around the same time Mafiaboy was apprehended, the FBI swooped down on a New Hampshire teenager known as Coolio, who boasted that he'd hacked into a number of Internet security companies and even into U.S. government Websites. In September 2000, a fifteen-year-old New Jersey youth, Jonathon Lebed, became the first minor to be charged with fraud by the U.S. Securities and Exchange Commission for online stock rigging. These teens are just the latest in a long line of high-tech hackers dating back to the mid-eighties. That's when seventeen-year-old Kevin Mitnick (aka Condor) developed the tactic of "phone phreaking" — breaking into and tampering with telephone company computers. Mitnick was once arrested for hacking into the U.S. Pentagon's computer system. He served nearly five years in prison.

Obviously, the fact that many kids have greater expertise than most adults in dealing with new technologies doesn't necessarily mean they have the maturity or life experience to handle what they encounter. At the same time, because of the generation gap in computer literacy, kids spend their time on the Net largely unsupervised. Most parents are basically clueless about the Internet, or they are too busy to monitor their kids, or a combination of both. But this disconnection has only exaggerated parents' fears, and for many of them, the Internet has become the new electronic bogeyman, with Web porn replacing TV violence as the great threat to childhood.

Patrolling the Web

Microsystems, a Boston-based manufacturer of computer software, liked to bill its Cyber Patrol as the "World's Most Trusted Internet Filtering Solution." But that was before the company met up with Matthew Skala, a twenty-three-year-old graduate student of computer science living in Victoria, British Columbia. He is a self-described crusader for the intellectual freedom of young people and an opponent of filtering systems, which he calls censorware. Since Microsystems, like most providers of this kind of software, refuses to make public its list of blocked sites, Skala and a colleague, Eddy Jansson, designed a program that would allow them to see what the software was denying access to. They discovered, among other things, that Cyber Patrol wouldn't load sites dedicated to anti–nuclear activism and even some fireworks manufacturers under its Militant/Extremist category. Under the heading of Cult/Satanic, the list targeted anything pertaining to atheism — including the official site of the Canadian Broadcasting Company, because it contained a news item about atheism. Skala and Jansson even found that sites criticizing Microsystems' parent company, Mattel (of Barbie fame), were being blocked by Cyber Patrol.

When they publicized their findings on Skala's Website, Microsystems and Mattel promptly slapped a lawsuit on them. Realizing they were facing a protracted and costly legal battle, Skala and Jansson settled out of court, which included an agreement to sell their program to Microsystems for one dollar. In its public statements, the company tried to paint the pair as ordinary vandal/hackers, but on his Website, Skala makes it clear that his intent wasn't mischief-making. It was to expose the arbitrary nature of Cyber Patrol's list of censored sites. Skala's battle with Microsystems was only the latest in a long line of skirmishes between Internet blocking services and free-speech-minded Webheads. A few years earlier, for example, Bennett Haselton, an eighteen-year-old student at Vanderbilt University, was similarly scared off by the threat of a lawsuit when he took on the makers of another popular blocking agent, CYBERsitter.

Skala and Haselton may be outraged by blocking software, but their libertarian sentiments aren't shared by an awful lot of parents. Their nervousness about the relative ease with which kids navigate the Net has made parents all too ready to turn over the monitoring of their children's online behavior to outside agents. Since the mid-nineties, these parental anxieties have fuelled the rapid rise of an entire industry devoted to blocking software. Most of the providers draw up their own blacklists, refusing to make these public, or to explain how they're arrived at, beyond vague guidelines and references to community standards. But who decides which sites are inappropriate, and on what basis? CYBERsitter, for example, blocked access to the National Organization of Women (NOW) Website because of its references to lesbians, as well as to a number of AIDS-information Web pages, and even to the Godiva chocolates site (maybe they were worried there'd be pictures of nude women on horseback, slathered in dark chocolate). Another filtering system blocked access to a site operated by an advocacy group for religious tolerance because it mentioned the word prostitute. One online free-speech group, Peacefire, has surveyed a number of filtering programs, finding numerous examples of inappropriately blocked sites, including human rights advocacy Web pages and a good deal of neutral, inoffensive material.

More recently, newer products have come along that are more sophisticated than the first wave of blocking software. While Cyber Patrol, CYBERsitter and Net Nanny act somewhat like V-chips for computers, blocking access to pre-selected channels, these newer programs take things up a notch. Anti–virus providers like Norton Internet Security have begun to add parental-control features to their firewall software. Norton's NIS 2000 Family Edition gives parents the ability to monitor their kids' surfing habits as well as to block access to particular sites. SurfMonkey and JuniorNet, both of which went on the market in 1999, set up closed environments on the Web, ensuring that the only content kids can get is from approved sources. In essence, when users are hooked up to this kind of software, much as they might feel like they're on the Internet, they're actually one step removed from it. They may not even realize they're missing out on anything because, unlike kids whose computers have had blocking software installed, "Access Denied" doesn't appear on the screen in these closed Web portals.

Online safety of children is a real concern, however. As Sherry Turkle points out in *Life on the Screen,* the Net has brought a new fluidity to the concept of identity. In the anonymity of chat rooms, some people construct whole new identities — changing their names, genders and ages to suit the persona they choose to adopt at any given moment. This fluidity holds exciting possibilities for freeing us from stereotypes of sex, race and age, but it also has a dark side. The Net has created unprecedented and worrisome opportunities for online stalking of children. In the anonymity of cyberspace, adults are able to visit sites popular with kids and masquerade as children themselves. Since the popularity of the Net took off in the early nineties, there have been numerous cases of sex offenders using chat rooms to connect with kids, and in some cases arranging face-to-face meetings.

Consequently, some adults are taking a whole other approach to protecting children on the Web. Adapting a kind of neighborhood-watch model, an informal network of Internet patrollers has sprung up to combat online stalkers and sexual predators. When these computer-savvy volunteers come across either potential predators or child pornography, they alert law-enforcement authorities and turn over whatever evidence they've gathered. One of the largest Internet patrol groups, Cyberangels, is an offshoot of the Guardian Angels, who first gained fame — and notoriety — when they began vigilante-style patrols of the New York subway system more than two decades ago. Nevertheless, there's an important distinction to be made between kids reading dirty words and looking at dirty pictures — which is what filtering programs are meant to prevent — and kids being lured and manipulated by cyber-stalkers, who are the main target of these Internet patrol groups.

Parents who turn to filtering software are understandably trying to protect their children from harm. Many say their chief worry is that kids will accidentally click on graphic sexual images and other material they're not ready to handle. Of course for some kids, stumbling across porn isn't the issue. They're actively *looking* for it. The Internet is the modern-day equivalent of looking up dirty words in the dictionary and hiding copies of *Playboy* under the mattress. And despite the presence of porn and other repugnant material on the Net, some parents conclude that the negatives of filtering outweigh the positives. After carefully considering the issue, Don Tapscott and his wife decided against using blocking software on their family computer. They didn't want to turn over control to an outside agency that may not share their values. As he points out in *Growing Up Digital,* "Filtering software not only cuts out materials on sex, violence and drugs, it may also block political, religious, and environmental issues that depict harsher realities."[5]

Still, large numbers of parents continue to put their faith in blocking programs, and political pressure for compulsory Internet filtering is growing. In 2000, the U.S. government established a special commission to consider whether schools and libraries that receive federal funding should be required to install filters. The move was ultimately rejected because, the commission concluded, existing technologies were just not up to the job. What the commission didn't question, however, was the ethics of filtering and the protectionist philosophy it's based on. Filtering software and closed-environment programs try to re-erect the walled garden of childhood in cyberspace, shielding kids from (possibly) harmful influences, but also barring them from the richness and diversity of the Web.

Many computer-savvy observers argue that filtering may work in the short run, but that denying kids access to the full range of the Internet doesn't really serve them — or society — well in the long run. Jon Katz sees it as a children's rights issue, part of a new social contract emerging between adults and children. In his view, "The young have a moral right of access to the machinery and content of media and culture."[6] Both Katz and Tapscott agree that there are real hazards in cyberspace, but argue that it's the job of adults to street-proof kids so they'll understand the dangers, learn to trust their instincts, and seek adults' help when they need to. Writing about the controversy on his Website, Matthew Skala uses a similar analogy:

> If you want to protect someone from disease, you don't do it by
> sealing them in a sterile plastic bubble away from all possible
> sources of infection. You do it by allowing them to build up
> immunities to low-level pathogens in their environment, possibly
> even getting sick from time to time. Then when they encounter a
> more serious potential infection, they're better prepared to defend

themselves ... Only children who can experience the full range of human thought will be able to develop the critical thinking skills, the mental immune systems they need to survive. [7]

The Virtual Mall

Meanwhile, another kind of predatory influence lurks in cyberspace, completely unregulated and impervious to most blocking software. In a few short years, the Internet has gone from being an anarchic network of academics and computer geeks to a sea of brand-name billboards, a vast virtual mall of advertising and online shopping. Though few people can summon up the same degree of indignation about commercialization as they do about porn, there is increasing concern about the untrammeled opportunities the Web offers for marketing directly to children.

The issue has been festering since the mid-nineties, with the controversy over the pervasive advertising on children's Websites. One example of this was a self-described "educational playground" offering art programs and interactive games. KidsCom gained instant popularity with its Keypals feature, which offered children the opportunity to have online penpals. But when some curious parents checked out the site, they found that every click of the mouse led to a series of questions clearly meant for market-research purposes: "How many people live in your house?" "What's your favorite TV commercial?" "Do you have an e-mail address, and what is it?" For answering the questions, kids could collect KidsKash points to redeem for free prizes from sponsoring companies like Gatorade. Another way to win KidsKash was by getting new kids to log on and sign up. This site came under fire from the Washington-based Center for Media Education, which accused its creators of misrepresenting itself as educational and misleading the kids who visited it. KidsCom subsequently cleaned up its act by adopting an "ad bug" to distinguish advertising from the so-called educational content.

(Naturally, this icon is irresistibly cute, and kids are all too eager to follow wherever it leads.)

Meanwhile, those who prefer their commercialism up front have only to log on to major sites like Disney.com. Since the late nineties, Hagen Joergensen has fought a valiant one-man campaign against the advertising-laden site. Joergensen, who is Denmark's official consumer watchdog, claims that it violates the Danish Marketing Practices Act, which explicitly forbids "sales promotions addressed to, or likely to influence children" and which "take advantage of their natural credulity or lack of experience." Disney retorted that it didn't have to obey Danish laws and that its revenue from that country (with its population of only 5 million and — the horror! — no Disney retail store in Copenhagen) was small potatoes anyway. But ever aware of maintaining its family-friendly image, the company was still stung by the charge. As a spokesperson told The *Wall Street Journal,* "We are stellar examples of how companies should interact with children."

But Joergensen and others are fighting a losing battle. Marketers know full well that, for the most part, kids are surfing solo. Online marketing and gathering of consumer data — both directly and via the use of tracking markers known as "cookies" — has become part and parcel of Websites aimed at children. The most recent trend in shopping sites is the virtual wallet, in which a parent can deposit funds in an account in a child's name, which she or he can then use to purchase things on the site. Some parents think these online accounts are a great idea because they encourage kids to budget and take independent responsibility for their purchases. But others say it's just one more way retailers and marketers are doing an end run around parents, creating a new generation of shopaholics. The Children's Online Privacy Protection Act, a U.S. law that requires Websites to get written parental permission before they obtain e-mail addresses and other information from kids under thirteen, came into effect early in 2000. But Disney.com and most of the other big sites had already begun doing so in anticipation of the law.

The explosive growth of Internet shopping explains why eleven- to nineteen-year-old girls are one of the Web's most sought-after demographics. The increasing presence of pop idols on the Web will boost the already powerful lure of online shopping for kids. In 2000, singer Britney Spears signed on to become the public face of Canada-based Youtopia, a youth-oriented e-business. The pop star announced that she was looking forward to the chance to "check out hip clothes, chat and hang out at virtual parties" with fans on the site. Youtopia, meanwhile, intends to gather marketing data from kids who visit, and reward them with loyalty points they can use to purchase products advertised on the site.

Clearly, the Web is open for business. Kids who can afford to are flocking to the virtual mall, and there's only so much that parents can do about it. More than any other group, tweens are the hot demographic *du jour*, representing the promise of new marketing opportunities. In fact, they're playing much the same role in the economy as teenagers did back in the post–war boom of the fifties.

NOTES

1. Anne Wood, presented to the Second World Summit on Television for Children, London, England, March 11, 1998.
2. Jon Katz, *Virtuous Reality: How America Surrendered Discussion of Moral Values to Opportunists, Nitwits and Blockheads like William Bennett* (New York: Random House, 1997), 173.
3. Michelle Slatalla, "How Young is Too Young for Technology?" *The Globe and Mail* (21 June 1999), C9.
4. Marguerite Holloway, "An Ethnologist in Cyberspace," *Scientific American* (April 1998), 30.
5. Don Tapscott, *Growing Up Digital: The Rise of the Net Generation* (New York: McGraw-Hill, 1998), 243.
6. Jon Katz, "The Rights of Kids in the Digital Age," *Wired* (July 1996), p. 123.
7. "Cyber Patrol Break FAQ." Matthew Skala's Home Page. http://www.islandnet.com/~mskala/cpbgaq.html.

TEEN RITES AND WRONGS

BACK WHEN I WAS IN MY TWENTIES and far from even contemplating becoming a parent, I met a woman at a party whose daughter was just entering her teenage years. The woman was very upset about the changes she was witnessing in her daughter's personality. "She's not the person I knew," the mother said. "She's turned into someone else." "How is she different?" I asked. Her complaints were very specific: her daughter had become angry, demanding and unpleasant, where once she had been unfailingly compliant and good-natured. The mother said she wished her daughter would revert back to her former self, and made it clear — to me and, no doubt, to her daughter as well — that she wanted nothing to do with this "other person."

The woman's attitude rankled me, for reasons that I had trouble putting my finger on at the time. How did she know this "other person" wasn't a side of her daughter's personality that she hadn't seen before? It seemed to me almost as if on some level she was disowning her own kid. But who was I to judge? I didn't have kids. What did I know?

Well, I know now. I've been on the receiving end of other person syndrome with Martha, my older daughter. As she moved into her teens, there were days when our once-easy relationship was fraught with tension, days when I felt silently accused of god-knows-what, days when no matter what I did or said, I was wrong. At times it really did seem as though some alien force had taken over her body, and I can remember wondering which version of my daughter would wake up in the morning. Martha is a young adult now, living mostly away from home, and when we see one another we get along swimmingly. But there is the small matter of her younger sister, poised on the brink ...

We all know the drill: the collective groans when a parent mentions that his or her child has just turned thirteen, the joking comments about raging hormones and how we wish we could ship 'em off to a desert island till it's over and they become human again. Of course it's true that teenagers can be very difficult to live with, that they're no longer the sweet, compliant children they once were. But even though I understand better just what that woman at the party was talking about, I realize now why her attitude still bugs me. Because I think it's a kind of verbal shorthand for what's wrong with our collective attitude toward teenagers. We've come to see adolescents as, at worst, a scourge, or more mercifully (we think), as walking catalogues of problems that we then earnestly seek to solve.

During the first decade of the 21st century, teenagers will make up a greater proportion of the population than ever before. If we don't start coming to grips with this, we're in for some real trouble. Because it's in the teen years that the chickens come home to roost, that the consequences and contradictions of keeping children in a separate sphere, a walled garden, become glaringly evident. The developed world is faced with teeming masses of young people — many of whom are sullen, bored and suspicious of adults, and have no power except the power to buy, to be consumers. Even though in many ways — sexually, intellectually, economically — they're functioning on a level equivalent to that of adults, we still hold them at bay, refusing to let them take their place in the grown-up world. Then suddenly, magically, the door swings open at the end of high school. They're like long-time prisoners abruptly let free with no period of parole, no chance to get acclimatized to their newly free status. Then we wonder why many of them are anti-social and so ill-equipped to deal with the world.

Just who is the problem here, them, or us?

The Invention of the Terrible Teens

They have execrable manners, flaunt authority, have no respect for their elders. They no longer rise when their parents or teachers enter the room. What kind of awful creatures will they be when they grow up? [1]

The troublesome adolescent has, to some extent, always been with us, as these words of Socrates from the fourth century BC show. But the figure of the troubled adolescent that we're more familiar with now is of more recent vintage, and didn't really begin to emerge until the Romantic period. The protagonist of Goethe's wildly popular 18th-century novel *The Sorrows of Young Werther,* for example, certainly prefigures the modern-day teenager with his mood swings, suicidal thoughts and tortured romantic longings. Half a century later, Wagner premiered *Siegfried.* In *Centuries of Childhood,* author Philippe Ariès calls the opera's hero the "first typical adolescent of modern times."[2] The teenager, like the notion of childhood itself, is largely a latter-day invention. The term "teen-age" didn't make its first appearance in English until the twenties, and it took another couple of decades for "teenager" (now minus the hyphen) to pass into popular usage. Throughout most of Western history, in fact, the distinction between childhood and adulthood was not nearly as sharp as we make it today. For the most part, a young person came to be considered an adult simply by taking on the appropriate trappings and responsibilities, which mainly meant marriage and children. The onset of puberty, far from marking the beginning of the preparatory period we now call adolescence, was intrinsically acknowledged as the beginning of adulthood.

It was the publication of psychologist G. Stanley Hall's book *Adolescence* in 1904 that firmly established the belief that adolescence is something akin to the terrible teens. Hall's book had a huge impact when it was published, and his view of the teenage years as a psychologically tumultuous period beset with perils and problems set the tone for the cultural view of teens that persists to this day. The essence of Hall's message is that teenagers need to be prevented from growing up too fast, that their inner turmoil needs to be tamed and channelled into productive, mature pursuits. And not surprisingly, much of his litany of risks and problems focused on their emerging sexuality, a legacy of the Victorian attitude toward sex. This anxiety about sex and young people continued to play itself out through the first half of the twentieth century, from the flap about flappers and flaming youth in the twenties right up to the outrage that greeted Elvis's explosion onto the scene in the fifties. But though Hall was the first to give a psychological framework to adolescent turmoil, he was far from being the first to point to teenagers as a disruptive influence on society.

In historian Norbert Schindler's study of the boys' societies, or *knabenschaften,* of 16th-century Switzerland, there is behavior echoed by today's out-of-control youth These former groups operated much like urban gangs — staking out territories and fighting with rival gangs in neighboring cantons. The roving bands of young males were the masters of the night, launching attacks on property and occasionally lapsing into violence. Many complaints about them focused on the practice of (yes, really) yodeling, which was the 16th-century equivalent of kids squealing their tires or turning the volume of their boomboxes up on the subway.

Youthful rebellion isn't always of the anarchic variety, however. From the fundamentalist Puritan youth movement known as the Great Awakening in 18th-century New England to the revolutionary purity of Mao's Red Guards in the seventies, there are abundant examples of youth who zealously support the prevailing values and challenge their elders to live up to them. But these various youth movements are all disruptive in one way or another. For while the adult impulse is to maintain order and stability, the teenage impulse is toward excitement and experience: toward instability.

Still, most of these youthful disruptions and rebellions were eventually tamed and absorbed into the cultural mainstream. As much as grown-ups may have railed against the yodeling and the other nocturnal antics of the *knabenschaften*, for example, overall there was an attitude of relaxed tolerance. Adults in 16th-century Switzerland exhibited the same indulgence toward youthful misbehavior as most societies do, viewing it as a normal and self-limiting part of growing up. But, as Schindler himself notes, something has changed. No longer is there the assumption that it's just a stage that will calm down with maturity. Instead, teenagers have become our collective cultural nightmare.

How did we get to the point where our kids scare the living daylights out of us?

Barbarians at the Gates

As I mentioned in Chapter Three, Frederic Wertham was the first in a long line of experts to try to pin the blame for youthful misbehavior on popular media. *Seduction of the Innocent,* his 1954 attack on comic books, set off a national wave of panic about juvenile delinquency, and its language and tone are strikingly similar to today's rhetoric. Hard as it is to believe that anyone could attribute such near-demonic powers to bits of colored paper, adults in the fifties seized on the idea of banning the books in much the same way as parents nowadays call for crackdowns on rap lyrics and violent video games. The fifties also witnessed the arrival of an entire genre of teen rebel movies, typified by *The Wild One*, in which Marlon Brando plays the sullen leader of a motorcycle gang. When asked, "What are you rebelling against?" he replies with a threatening sneer, "What d'ya got?" Today, *The*

Wild One looks a bit dated, and the term juvenile delinquency sounds quaint. But aside from the terminology, not much has changed. We're still gripped by the same fear and loathing when it comes to young people, manifesting itself as widespread hysteria over youth crime. A daily diet of headlines about teen violence spreads the view that high schools in North America are seething cauldrons, that roving gangs of teenagers terrorize people in shopping malls and that the criminal justice system is hopelessly lenient on young offenders. Youth gangs, squeegee kids, Goths, ravers — they're the latter-day version of the barbarian hordes hovering at our gates, looking to destroy civilization as we know it.

It seems we need to *believe* things are worse than ever, that today's kids are bad apples, even when there's evidence to the contrary. People are convinced, for example, that violent crime among youth is way up, but there's no firm evidence that this is true. Some studies actually show a steady decline in youth crime in the past few decades. One difficulty in determining the extent of the problem is defining just what constitutes a crime. Certain activities that, in the past, were tolerated as youthful hijinks and dealt with by parents and school authorities now frequently result in criminal charges. The category of "youth crime" can encompass offences as serious as murder and as minor as writing graffiti in a public place. This debate, which is largely about statistics, shouldn't obscure the reality that transgressive behavior is a big part of youth culture. Teenagers *do* engage in violence, and when they do, it's usually directed against other teenagers rather than against adults. Ultimately, the widespread *perception* that youth crime is rising is just as significant as what the statistics actually say. The various waves of panic about youth crime over the past half-century reveal as much about the larger society as they do about teenagers themselves.

Panic and fear were almost palpable following the Littleton, Colorado shootings, in which Eric Harris and Dylan Klebold killed twelve students and one teacher at Columbine High School before turning their guns on themselves. For weeks after the massacre, the news media were obsessed with various Hollywood explanations. Klebold and Harris were said to be aping *The Matrix,* for example, because, like the Keanu Reeves character in the film, they favored long black trench coats. Some pundits speculated that the massacre was triggered by *The Basketball Diaries,* in which Leonardo DiCaprio's character fantasizes about going on a shooting rampage in his school. Others pointed to the 1989 black comedy *Heathers,* in which a twisted youth hatches a plot to blow up his high school. In subsequent weeks, the paranoia about some kind of pop-culture infection was sustained by a number of reported copycat shootings across North America. Even in the small town of Taber, Alberta, a student was gunned down in a school corridor.

These crimes help to build a growing movement to try very young offenders in adult courts, reversing the trend toward a separate justice system for juveniles, which has prevailed for the better part of the past century. In one of the most extreme examples, an eleven-year-old Michigan youth was tried as an adult and convicted of murder in 1999. This increasing pressure on the courts to get tough with young offenders only serves to muddy the underlying issue: is youth crime better dealt with as a legal problem or as a social problem? But the political currency of youth crime is just too attractive. Like TV and video-game violence, it's another convenient scapegoat, ready to be brought out when governments need to score political points without actually having to *do* anything.

I don't have far to look to see the phenomenon in action. Over the past few years, whenever the governing party in Ontario wants to bolster its popularity, it can be counted on to trot out such things as boot camps for young offenders and compulsory school uniforms. The latter is a favorite with many adults, who seem to believe that if high school students dress like fifties kids, they'll somehow magically behave like fifties kids. (I'll concede that there's a valid argument to be made in favor of uniforms. For instance, there's the claim that wearing uniforms helps reduce the peer pressure kids feel regarding labels. Personally, I've never met a high school student who bought that argument, though. Some other advocates of uniforms claim that they actually make schools safer by helping to readily identify intruders, an argument that only underscores the extent of the siege mentality that exists in many schools today.)

The result of all this is the wholesale stigmatization of an entire segment of the population. A 1999 survey of more than 2,000 young people in Toronto found that only a third felt they get respect and less than half felt welcome in their own home city. Even "good" kids feel marginalized and discriminated against when they go into corner stores or take public transit. It seems that young people are one group that can be insulted with impunity: it's so automatic that we aren't even conscious we're doing it. When hockey legend Maurice "Rocket" Richard died in 2000, one woman was quoted in *The Toronto Star,* "If our youth had one-hundredth of his spunk, what a country we would have." A high school teacher leapt to their defence in a letter to the editor: "I am mystified," she wrote, "as to why anyone would make such a sweeping and prejudicial comment about our young citizens." The ultimate irony is that so much of the demonization of today's kids comes from members of the baby-boom generation. The same people who used to say "never trust anyone over thirty" now seem to have little use for anyone under twenty.

The Woodstock '99 festival offered an excellent example of how the media help foster this negative view. I'm old enough to remember the coverage of the original Woodstock, which was full of stories about bad drug trips and images of long-haired, mud-smeared, half-naked hippies. Thirty years later, the 1969 festival has been romanticized as the embodiment of peace and love, while the kids who attended Woodstock '99 were portrayed as thugs and pyromaniacs, betrayers of the ideals of the original event. Thankfully, not everyone buys into this view: Oscar-winning documentary filmmaker Barbara Kopple believes that the '99 festival was much closer to the spirit of the original Woodstock than media reports suggested. When her documentary *My Generation* was screened at the 2000 Toronto Film Festival, Kopple stressed in an interview that both concerts were about young people showing "a sense of community and a sense of ritual." Her film documents that much of the so-called vandalism of Woodstock '99 had a clearly political motivation:

> No one got hurt. The non-profit tents, nobody broke into those. They gave away the clothes they took from the vendors and tents that were totally overpriced. They smashed the ATM's. It was almost full circle from 1969 ... to 1999.[3]

Whether we're devouring our own young, like Cronos, or simply disowning them, these attitudes are a revealing barometer of how little faith we have in our own future. But not all the images of young people today are negative ones. In fact, a whole different view of adolescence pops up in some surprising places.

Images of Initiation

In certain parts of our pop culture landscape, adolescence is associated with the emergence of powerful forces for good. It's fascinating to look at the teenage superhero genre in this regard. On the TV shows *Mighty Morphin Power Rangers, Teenage Mutant Ninja Turtles* and *Sailor Moon,* the characters are teenagers who have the ability to transform themselves into beings with superhuman powers. In these stories, the superhero is a metaphor for the coming-into-power that's *supposed* to happen at adolescence, which is why they show these characters undergoing a metamorphosis into another life form altogether. Consider the young mutant teenager Jubilee, from the *X-Men* comics and TV series. She frets over her inability to control the changes her body is going through as her special powers begin to assert themselves. This kind of transformation is actually a wonderfully apt way to describe the enormous physical and emotional changes of adolescence. Jubilee feels like an outcast, and longs to be normal. "I didn't ask to be a mutant!" she cries, which could be the lament of any adolescent. In 2001, Marvel Comics introduced *Ultimate X-Men*, an updated version of the series with a whole new roster of mutant teenagers battling against evil and learning to control their emerging superpowers.

Different kind of powers take hold of the teenage girls in occult-themed TV shows like *Buffy the Vampire Slayer* and *Charmed*, and movies like *The Craft*. In the latter, a quartet of girls decide to delve into traditional witchcraft practices, and discover powers they didn't know they had. The protagonist of *Buffy* discovers that she's been karmically chosen to be a vampire slayer, and she undergoes lengthy and rigorous training to carry out her mission. In all of these stories, the disruptive powers of adolescence are not seen as inherently negative or destructive. When these teen witches and superheroes are helped to channel their emerging abilities in the right direction, they become powerful forces for good. The main way this is done is through the influence of mentors, whose explicit role is to provide sympathetic but challenging guidance to the young heroes. There's Giles in *Buffy*, Professor Xavier in *X-Men*, Zordon the gigantic talking head in *Power Rangers*, and Splinter, the kindly old rat who helps the Ninja Turtles control their constant craving for pizza and other junk foods. These figures, and in fact the whole Teen Superhero genre itself, are inspired by ancient myths and age-old initiation practices that embody a very different approach to adolescence than our own.

In fact, many of the older tribal cultures are way ahead of us in this regard. Even though these societies don't have the same separation of the child and adult realms that prevails in the modern world, their traditional rites of initiation acknowledge that the entry into adulthood has significance for the individual and for the society as a whole. Initiation has both social and spiritual dimensions that embrace raw, wild adolescent energies rather than clamping down on them. These rites of passage vary considerably from culture to culture, but there are certain common elements. Typically, the young people are isolated from society for a period of time, which is frequently achieved by going into the wilderness, as in the vision quests of various North American Native tribes and the walkabouts of the Australian aborigines. Often they are given difficult, sometimes life-threatening tasks to perform, and they may receive symbolic body markings from tribal elders, a practice followed by many of the tribes in central Africa. The rituals may also involve the use of herbs, drugs or fasting, which are meant to evoke altered states of consciousness. Young males are the focus of most of the initiation rituals documented in the anthropological literature, but many tribal societies also have analogous rites for girls on the occasion of their first menstrual period.

Interestingly, this description of traditional initiation bears some striking similarities to the behavior we observe in modern teenagers — the danger-seeking, the separation from adult society, even the body-marking in the form of piercings and tattoos. It also helps explain why teens are so drawn to drugs and alcohol, and why the Just Say No approach has been so ineffective. Kids are keenly aware of many parents' hypocrisy, glossing over their own past experiences with drugs and blithely advocating a philosophy of "Do as I say, not as I did." Without an understanding of the appeal of mind-altering experiences, and of the spiritual role they play in the initiation process, we can't help kids identify what it is they're really looking for when they take drugs.

This notion of initiatory behavior also applies to one of the thorniest issues of all: teenage smoking. Despite decades of propaganda about its dire health consequences, public health experts increasingly acknowledge that the danger model has been singularly unsuccessful in discouraging young teens from smoking. This was borne out by a fifteen-year study of more than 8,000 high school students carried out by the U.S. National Cancer Institute, which showed that kids who participated in intensive smoking prevention programs were just as likely to take up the habit as kids who didn't.

When the results of the NCI study were published toward the end of 2000, they seemed to be the final nail in the coffin of traditional anti-smoking campaigns. It's not all that hard to see why this approach has been such a spectacular failure with teenagers, who usually greet these scaremongering ads with hoots of derisive laughter. Not only do they think they're being condescended to, but they reject the message outright. Playing on fears isn't effective with teens, precisely because they're not afraid of the things we think they should be. This is what a lot of danger-seeking behavior is really all about: it's in teens' cultural DNA to push things to the limit, and it may well be the very thing they need to do to fully grow up.

Kids may be reluctant to listen to what adults are telling them about the dangers of drugs and smoking, but that doesn't mean they don't need our guidance. Initiation is not something young people can do for themselves. In most societies, adult involvement is considered crucial, because the process is too fraught with dangers — both physical and psychological — to be left to the young. But it's important to point out that, in many ways, parents are the *least* appropriate people to guide their children through initiation. To achieve true adulthood, kids have to psychologically leave home, to break away from the influence of their parents and find their own way in the world. Through these rites, adults are supposed to provide structure, boundaries, a kind of safe container for the extreme emotions young people experience during this period of life.

Traditional societies view initiation not as a private, family matter, but as a social mechanism for which the entire community takes responsibility. Implicit in this is an acknowledgement that nothing is more vital to a society's well-being than the task of helping each new generation take its place in the world. Unfortunately, in our culture, there's a vacuum where this responsibility should be: adults in contemporary society are largely abdicating their roles as guides in the process of initiation. Like the bumbling, clueless grown-ups in so many teen comedies, many of us are no help, or are absent altogether. But in abdicating this responsibility, we're abandoning young people to their own devices. We're in essence forcing them to try to initiate themselves.

Kids Just Wanna Be Productive

It's a startling but little-remarked-upon fact that large numbers of teenagers now live the vast majority of their waking hours without any meaningful contact with adults. Yes, they see school principals and a host of other authority figures in the course of a day. The lucky ones develop bonds with sympathetic relatives, neighbors, teachers and others. But outside their families, teens encounter relatively few adults who knew them as children, or who are interested in them as individuals. By the same token, many adults have little or no contact with teenagers. Even parents often have little to do with teens other than their own, which helps explain their readiness to blame their kids' misbehavior on the bad influence of others. This alienation from kids extends to youth culture itself. Grown-ups may have some familiarity with pre-teen preoccupations like Pokémon and the Spice Girls, but when it comes to teen movies and hip-hop music, most of them are utterly clueless. It's completely foreign territory. Of course, teens want to have a culture all their own, and they should have one. But this extreme disconnection from the adult world makes teenagers a "tribe apart," as journalist Patricia Hersh describes them in her 1999 book of the same name. Alienation clearly played a role in the Littleton tragedy. Columbine High School is a huge suburban school of several thousand students. Dylan Klebold and Eric Harris were able to stockpile an arsenal of weapons and plan a massacre in the seclusion of their bedrooms, unbeknownst even to their families. Just as importantly, their isolation allowed them to nurse festering resentments against classmates without any teacher or other adult at Columbine intervening or even noticing.

The large warehouse-style high schools that we see in Canada and the U.S. today came with the post–war boom. Even into the early 20th century, teenagers were treated as young adults, and the majority of them didn't go to school after the eighth grade. High school did for teens what the establishment of elementary schools had done for younger children some 200 years earlier in Europe: it removed them *en masse* from the mainstream of life and isolated them in an institution of their own. In the case of high school, it also created the conditions for the development of a separate youth culture — clothes, music, slang. As I discussed earlier, marketers in the fifties seized on this emerging youth culture to exploit the new teenage consumer demographic. In less than a century, high school has come to be viewed as an inevitable, intrinsic part of teenage life — almost a state of nature. But for the first time since the education debates of the sixties and early seventies, a radical rethinking of high school is once again being seriously proposed.

One critic, Thomas Hine, argues that high school not only keeps teens in a state of enforced infantilism, it actually helps promote their consumerist tendencies. In his 1999 book, *The Rise and Fall of the American Teenager*, Hine suggests that the rebellious and disruptive behavior we've come to expect from teenagers may be neither a normal nor an inevitable part of adolescence. The problem, in Hine's view, stems from our treatment of adolescence as an extension of childhood, and of teenagers as a special subgroup rather than as what he calls beginner adults. Hine proposes the novel idea that what teenagers really want is not to lie around, cut classes and shop till they drop, but to be productive members of society. His ideas echo arguments made several decades earlier by anthropologist Margaret Mead and educator John Holt, who both believed that the young want to be useful. Early-childhood-education pioneer Maria Montessori had made a similar point about very young children with her well-known maxim that "play is the child's work."

From its very inception, Hine notes, high school was seen as an institution of social control, less about education than socialization. The true purpose of high school was to keep young people off the streets and, more importantly, out of the work force, where they would be competing with adults for jobs. By putting young people in vast warehouse-style schools, we reinforce their sense of marginality. This stands in stark contrast to the way youth were treated in the past, and the way they still are in many cultures. Teens used to be economically useful. Nowadays, their only role in society is to prepare for adulthood, and to be good consumers while doing it. One of the few remaining ways we allow them any sense of power over their lives is to give them the choice of what to buy and what not to buy. In a real sense, we're the ones who've made young people into, in Hine's phrase, "the monstrous progeny of marketing and high school."

There have been some efforts to humanize high schools. In recent decades they've become less regimented and authoritarian, with a general loosening of rules and dress codes, for instance. But though teachers and administrators have less power than they used to, they're also, with some exceptions, less involved in their students' lives. Many students find there's no adult at their school who knows them in a personal way, a fact that's encouraged the growth of the cultural gulf between adults and teenagers.

So is the answer to throw open the gates, to let teens stream out of high school and into dead-end McJobs? No. But if we're going to keep pressuring kids to stay in school, we had better start figuring out ways to lessen that alienation and make the institution more responsive to their needs. The thrust behind the creation of high school, like the invention of adolescence itself, was initially a positive one. It was supposed to create a breathing space, allowing for a period of preparation before young people took on the full responsibilities of adulthood. But in its present form, what high school mostly does is simply prolong childhood. By keeping teens so long in a state where their lives are effectively on hold, we deny them meaningful ways to feel useful in the present.

Teenagers constantly complain that adults treat them like children, demanding to know: "When are you going to start treating me like an adult?" Which raises the very questions we need to grapple with: When should childhood end? What is maturity? Just when does a person become an adult? A lot of our current problems stem from the fact that too often, the answer to that question is: *Never.* A lot of kids never really step into adulthood. We don't pave the way for them. We don't initiate them. In many ways, we actively thwart their efforts to grow up.

Some well-meaning adults, influenced by New Age ideas, argue that we should take our cue from tribal cultures, and adopt their traditional rites of initiation for our own children. (I've been guilty of this myself. Then I began to notice that, as much as I and my feminist friends would go all warm and fuzzy at the thought of having a ceremony to mark our daughters' first menstrual periods, the girls themselves would head for the hills as soon as the subject came up.) Lifting rites out of their cultural context and transplanting them wholesale into ours doesn't really do the job. As with so many aspects of modern life, we're heading into uncharted territory, trying to cobble together a new way of dealing with adolescence that draws on ancient wisdom, but still fits contemporary realities.

From the time they were nine years old, both our kids have spent a good chunk of their summers at a wilderness canoe camp in northern Ontario. Canoe tripping is emotionally and physically challenging, but our girls love their time at Wanapitei; in many ways their entire year revolves around it. Getting them to camp every summer has challenged our family finances. And some friends think we're nuts to shell out all that money so our kids can spend the summer lugging heavy packs over mosquito-infested, boulder-studded portages. But we've never doubted that it was worth it. Being in the wilderness offers the kids something we can't give them: the experience of initiation. Many organizations dealing with teenagers have started using this initiation model for personal growth, as well as an alternative to group homes and boot camps. For example, a Swiss organization, La Fontanelle, sends troubled kids on guided canoe trips in the northern Ontario bush.

Wilderness canoeing is only one model for initiation, and obviously it's not for everyone. Sports and the arts can also provide mentoring opportunities, as does the ancient model of apprenticeship. What all these endeavors do, in various ways, is to pose challenges, to allow young people the chance to take risks and go beyond their limitations in safe, structured ways. Fundamental to the whole process is that they be treated with respect, as the beginner adults they are. Whatever the road to initiation, it's vital that grown-ups reach out to help kids overcome their disconnection from the adult world. The task is to find ways for them to have personal relationships with elders who know them as people and give a shit about what happens to them. Adults *other* than their parents.

But that won't happen as long as we cling to the notion that parenting is the be-all and end-all in cross-generational relations.

NOTES

1. Socrates, in Michael Rosen, ed., *The Penguin Book of Childhood* (New York: Viking, 1994).
2. Philippe Ariès, *Centuries of Childhood,* translated from the French by Robert Baldick (New York: Vintage Books, 1962), 140-141.
3. Doug Saunders, "From the Flower Children to Generation X," *The Globe and Mail*, 14 September 2000, R3.

THE GREAT PARENTING DEBATE

WALK INTO ANY BOOKSTORE in North America and you'll see them: row upon row of books shelved in sections marked Family or Child Care or Parenting. Never mind the old saying. In the case of the books found in these aisles, you usually can tell exactly what they are by their covers:

> *My Teenager is Driving Me Crazy! ... Whining: 3 Steps to Stopping it Before the Tears and Tantrums ... Raising Your Child's Inner Self-Esteem ... Don't be Afraid to Discipline ... Parenting a Child with a Learning Disability ... The Tao of Parenting ...*

Name any aspect of parenting, and chances are somebody's written a book on it. There are even books for under-achievers *(Parenting for Dummies)* and over-achievers *(Hyper-parenting: Are You Hurting Your Children by Trying Too Hard?)*. Once, adults brought kids up. Nowadays we parent them. If there's one thing that characterizes contemporary family life, it's this preoccupation with parenting as a technique to be studied, a skill to be learned, a system to be mastered.

We didn't used to need all this printed advice (or at least we didn't know we did). Oh, sure, parents have always gone to relatives and friends for tips on how to treat a bad case of diaper rash, or called the doctor to ask how long to keep a child with chicken pox home from school. But as far as the social upbringing of children was concerned, people muddled along, doing things pretty much the way their parents had. In the first half of the 20th century there was a general — if largely unexamined — social consensus on child rearing. Babies were fed on rigidly timed schedules and toilet-trained as early as possible. Young children were hit when they were naughty. Adult authority was supreme. The only explanation a parent owed a child was "Because I said so."

But midway through the century, things began to change. This social consensus began to unravel, divorce and family breakdown became more common, and with the rise of the mass media, parents found they could no longer control the flow of information, ideas and images their children were exposed to. Raising children in this complicated world became a far more daunting task, and parents began to express new and unprecedented anxieties about their ability to do it properly. In the seventies, books dealing specifically with child rearing became one of the fastest-growing sectors of the publishing industry. The writers of parenting books became a kind of new priesthood. Bringing up children — once considered a natural, almost instinctual activity — was now considered the preserve of the Expert.

A Short History of Parenting Books

The granddaddy of them all was, of course, Dr. Spock. From its publication in 1946 until Benjamin Spock's death in 1999, *Baby and Child Care* had been published in more than 30 languages and sold over 50-million copies worldwide. *Baby and Child Care* was the first truly comprehensive manual on child rearing, and it's still one of the few that attempts to cover such a wealth of medical information and behavioral advice in one volume. And unlike many current child experts, Spock offered parents no systematized approach that could be neatly summed up in a few sound bites. The book is chatty and discursive, drawing on personal anecdotes as much as on child development theory. (In fact, the original title was *The Common Sense Book of Baby and Child Care.*)

Baby and Child Care is widely viewed as having ushered in a new era of permissiveness, and indeed, Spock departed from the prevailing orthodoxy of his day in many ways. He recommended on-demand feeding for infants and a tolerant attitude toward masturbation, for instance. But today Spock's advice sounds quite moderate and even-handed, delivered in a reassuring, even grandfatherly tone (though Spock himself was only in his forties when he first wrote it). He sees much of his job as one of reinforcing parents' instincts. Again and again he advises them to just do whatever feels comfortable: "Don't take too seriously all that the neighbors say. Don't be overawed by what the experts say. Don't be afraid to trust your own common sense. Bringing up your child won't be a complicated job if you take it easy and trust your own instincts." At times, Spock even suggests that, when in doubt, parents should just do things the way their parents did, advice that would be considered rather backward and unenlightened today. In some ways, what was truly radical about *Baby and Child Care* in its day was the idea that raising children wasn't this hyper-serious, weighty responsibility; it could actually be fun. Throughout the book, Spock is constantly exhorting parents to "enjoy your baby!" This advice was like a breath of fresh air among the rigid Victorian notions that still held sway in middle-class families.

For the better part of two decades, *Baby and Child Care* was the only game in town. But in the seventies, a different breed of child-rearing expert began to emerge. British psychologist Penelope Leach's *Your Baby and Child*, first published in 1977, became the handbook for a generation that considered Dr. Spock a bit old-fashioned, a bit too identified with their parents. Leach's approach was hardly a radical departure from Spock's, offering a similar mix of physical-care-and-feeding advice combined with Leach's own more seventies-flavored views on child development. Unlike *Baby and Child Care*, Leach's book doesn't attempt to cover the entire cycle of childhood, concentrating instead solely on the years from birth to age five. These pre-school years were increasingly becoming the focal point of new books on parenting, spurred on by the surge of interest in natural childbirth and a growing body of research into infant and toddler development.

Another author whose books were eagerly consumed by a new breed of committed, informed parents was Harvard pediatrician T. Berry Brazelton. His book *Infants and Mothers* helped popularize the notion that what happens in the first three years of life will determine a child's future (a theory now being challenged on a number of fronts, as I'll discuss a bit later). Brazelton became particularly well-known for his relaxed views on toilet-training. He advised parents to let the child decide when he or she is ready, ushering in a trend toward later toilet-training. More recently, Brazelton's views have come under attack from traditionalists. Author John Rosemond has compared toilet-training to housebreaking a puppy, saying that for children over the age of two to be wearing diapers is an insult to their intelligence. It didn't enhance Brazelton's credibility when, in the late nineties, he began to appear as a paid spokesperson for Pampers.

From the seventies onward, though, there was another school of thought — one that advocated a more structured, analytical approach to child rearing. An early and influential representative of this trend was psychologist Rudolf Dreikurs. His best-known book, *Children: The Challenge,* was first published in the sixties, but his ideas achieved greater prominence after his death in the early seventies. Dreikurs was a follower of psychoanalyst Alfred Adler, a contemporary of Freud whose theories emphasized the role of cognitive awareness and rational discussion in dealing with the problems of living. He pioneered the idea of quasi-democratic family councils, where parents and children could jointly map out such things as schedules of chores, and discuss any areas of disagreement calmly and rationally. Dreikurs' ideas were an early and important acknowledgement that the family was becoming a more democratic institution, that the era of "Because I said so" was coming to an end.

Nevertheless, it was also Dreikurs who re-introduced the concept of discipline into child rearing. For despite all the child-led philosophy, there was still the primary dilemma of parenthood: how do you get kids to do what you want them to do? Dreikurs' singular brilliance was to recast the notion of discipline into what he called logical consequences. Children were no longer to be punished for wrongdoing, but instead made to deal with the consequences of their behavior. In Dreikurs' scheme children could, for example, choose not to eat dinner, but it was their tough luck if they got hungry later on. Dreikurs acknowledged there were limits to his approach — it wasn't meant to create problems for other people or to endanger the child's health. Kids still had to wear their jackets and mittens on cold days, for example. Though Dreikurs' name is little known now, it was *Children: The Challenge* that made the idea of consequences part of the child-rearing lexicon (though when used by the back-to-basics crowd, it comes out sounding more like a euphemism for punishment, something Dreikurs himself never intended).

Another influential author from the seventies whose work is still in wide circulation is Thomas Gordon, author of *P.E.T.: Parent Effectiveness Training* and a slew of similarly named follow-up books. It was the "Parent Effectiveness Training" series that pioneered the notion of a child-rearing system with concrete rules and catchphrases. Like Dreikurs, Gordon believed in the value of discussion between kids and their parents, and he promoted a technique he called active listening to resolve conflicts. Gordon was opposed to punishment and parents misusing their power over children. A large part of the *PET* system's appeal came from its creator's ability to package the child-centered approach into a series of sound bites that combined psychological jargon with the language of business.

Perhaps the best-known representative of the liberal, child-led tradition is Barbara Coloroso, whose ideas on helping children develop self-control became influential in the eighties via her audio tapes and videos. More than anyone else, Coloroso is responsible for popularizing the notion of a time-out. Coloroso informs parents that they can tell kids to go to their room — not as a punishment, but to give them a chance to cool out and reflect. In the early nineties, Coloroso's book *Kids Are Worth It!* became a bestseller. The book's subtitle — *Giving Your Child the Gift of Inner Discipline* — conveys a sense of how Coloroso manages to mix warm-and-caring with just enough discipline, much like the "backbone" parent she celebrates in her book.

The wave of parenting books continued unabated into the nineties, written by lesser-known (and quickly forgotten) authors. Most of these books tried to have it both ways, advocating a middle-ground between permissiveness and traditional parental authority that echoed Dr. Spock's common-sense approach. In fact, the most striking thing about many parenting books is their essential sameness — of point of view and, especially, of jargon. The content of the advice seems to matter less than parents' need to draw on a source outside of themselves: experts who possess an authority that they no longer feel they have.

It was inevitable that other voices would come along to speak to that profound loss of confidence, and to reassure parents that traditional methods of discipline were back in style. In the late nineties, there was a shift away from the child-centered philosophy of the seventies and eighties. A flood of stories appeared in the media exposing how indulgent parents, spurred on by permissive experts going right back to Dr. Spock, had created a generation of monsters — pint-size megalomaniacs raised on a diet of touchy-feely psychobabble, who could twist adults around their little fingers. A new spate of parenting books appeared, bearing titles like *You Be the Kid, I'll Be the Parent* and the nasty but no doubt eye-catching *I Refuse to Raise a Brat!* (written by TV actress Marilu Henner). One of the most prominent advocates of traditional child-rearing practices to emerge in the nineties was John Rosemond, whose parenting workshops and books served up old-fashioned discipline in a nineties-style package.

Rosemond's words were like manna from heaven to many frustrated parents, who claimed that "soft" techniques just didn't work (meaning they didn't yield the desired degree of compliance from kids). Many of those parents had tried out the techniques once or twice, only to go back to more familiar ways. Time-outs, which had become part of liberal parents' standard repertoire, came under attack. Some experts claimed it had become just another form of punishment, while others, including Rosemond, denounced it as "wimp parenting." Even more rigidly systematized techniques gained in popularity, like psychologist Thomas Phelan's 1-2-3 Magic, in which the adult carries out an immediate and non-negotiable countdown to a time-out every time a child misbehaves.

None of this should have been surprising, because the child-centered philosophy went against the weight of centuries of Western culture. It has been viewed as the natural order that children should be under the absolute control of adults. Writers such as psychoanalyst Alice Miller have explored this dark underside of childhood. In her book, *For Your Own Good: Hidden Cruelty in Childrearing and the Roots of Violence,* Miller puts forth the radical notion that much of what are considered normal child-rearing practices actually constitute a socially sanctioned form of child abuse. But even if one doesn't accept this view, it's clear that our modern, "enlightened" attitudes toward children still haven't penetrated all that far into the culture. Indeed, what's most striking about the new liberal philosophies is how little impact they've had in real life. And nowhere is the gap between the child-development experts and ordinary people clearer than in the controversy that refuses to die: to spank or not to spank?

The Sound of One Hand Spanking

When Ivy was little, she and I would regularly indulge in something we called pretend spanking. Feigning anger, I'd tell her she'd been a bad girl, cover her behind with one of my hands and proceed to whack it with the other. Ivy would giggle as I pummelled away on my own hand, and when I was done she would inform me that it was a pretend spanking, not a real one. "Why do you say that?" I'd ask her. "Because," she'd announce triumphantly, "you put one hand down and you didn't spank, then you put the other hand down and you did spank!" It was one of those little family rituals — utterly baffling to outsiders, of course — that Ivy and I did with much enjoyment right through her toddler years. I realize now, though, that there was also a serious side to our little game. In some sense, it conveyed the tacit understanding between Ivy and me that "real" spanking was something that just didn't happen in our house.

Before going any further, I might as well go on the record: I'm against spanking and all forms of physical punishment. Always. In every instance. Zero tolerance. I've tried to get my head around the various arguments for and against, but to me the issue is so simple and obvious it's beyond discussion. For the life of me, I can't understand why it should be okay to do something to a child that would be considered assault if done to an adult. I think we should call spanking what it is: violence against the smallest, least powerful members of society. I look forward to the day when social and legal support for it is consigned to the dustbin of history, as slavery, foot-binding and wife-battering have been.

In this I actually find myself in agreement with the vast majority of parenting experts. But this is one area where their views don't cut much ice with the public at large. As readily as parents turn to experts about other matters, on the issue of corporal punishment, their advice is largely ignored. Polls on the subject turn up the same result time and again: roughly 70 per cent of North Americans view spanking as a legitimate form of discipline, whether or not they use it. But, as with so many issues related to children, public opinion on kids and violence is characterized by considerable ambivalence, if not outright confusion.

Take the controversy ignited back in the spring of 1997, when a father was charged with assault for pulling down his five-year-old daughter's underpants and giving her a spanking in a London, Ontario parking lot. Though witnesses described the man's actions as harsh and humiliating to the child, for weeks after the incident callers to phone-in shows were brimming with righteous indignation that he was being branded as a criminal for exercising his right as a parent. At the time, *The Toronto Star* ran a poll showing public opinion at more than 80 per cent in favor of spanking. Around the same time, the *Star* also ran the results of a poll on violence in the media. It showed that roughly the same percentage thought there was too much violence on television, and that the government should take steps to control it. Taken together, these two polls suggest what strikes me as a conundrum: most people seem to think that violence on TV is wrong, but that striking a child in real life is perfectly okay.

Though opponents of spanking haven't had much impact on public opinion, they have had considerable effect on the whole tone of the debate, to the extent that pro-spanking advocates often end up tying themselves in verbal knots to justify their position. Take one idea that's dear to the hearts of pro-spanking apologists: it shouldn't be done in anger, but coolly and calmly, lovingly even. But the idea of controlled spanking is a myth. Anger is precisely the trigger that gives rise to the urge to strike a child. Moreover, if the parent waits to hit the child *after* she or he has calmed down, it becomes almost a sinister, cold-blooded ritual. Still another popular argument is that of the "last resort," in which parents claim they only use spanking when all other disciplinary tactics have failed, or when nothing else will work. The usual example is to stop a toddler from running out into traffic. I can't remember the last time I heard of a child being spanked for running into traffic; I have seen tired, exasperated mothers haul off and whack fussy kids in shopping malls, though.

Which brings us to the "not too young, not too old" approach. When I was growing up, teenagers might get slapped or strapped with a belt, but children as old as eleven and twelve were routinely spanked on the buttocks without a second thought. But now that spanking is considered a teaching tool rather than a form of punishment, it's viewed as inappropriate to use on older children who can be reasoned with verbally. (There's also the realistic acknowledgment that, these days, older kids can't be "taught" to obey that way — and may well strike back.) Spanking doesn't teach babies either, who are cute and defenseless and can't understand why they're being hit. That leaves children between the ages of two and seven, who are old enough to walk and talk but not to reason (or hit back).

In his 1994 book, *To Spank or Not to Spank,* John Rosemond expends a lot of effort trying to show how spanking can be rational and humane. He maintains that it should always be done with an open hand, for instance (his own father used a belt on him). Interestingly, though Rosemond readily admits that past practices like his father's are no longer acceptable today, he never allows for the possibility that the same might be true for his own behavior. This passage gives the reader a sense of the mental gymnastics he employs:

> I did not spank on all ... occasions. Only sometimes. Selectively.
> When I felt like it. There was no science to my method, no calculation, psychology, or forethought. When I spanked, it was spontaneous, like the proverbial bolt out of the blue. But don't get me wrong. My spankings were definitely not impulsive, emotionally driven acts.
> I was in control, always, *using* my temper rather than *losing* it.[1]

While Rosemond's views aren't typical of the child development establishment, he's clearly in tune with the temper of the times. The case against corporal punishment — in particular the evidence that children who are spanked tend to be more aggressive and anti-social when they grow up — has been made persuasively in numerous studies. But the public just doesn't *buy* it. The persistence of spanking in the face of such broad-based rejection by child development professionals is a reflection of beliefs that are deeply embedded in our culture: that hitting is an inevitable and necessary part of raising a family; and that children are inherently wild, uncivilized creatures who must be molded and subjugated to the will of adults. Many people still can't imagine another way to deal with children. As one father told a reporter for *The Toronto Star,* "When you don't spank a child, if there is a standoff between a parent and a child, how does it get resolved?" In other words, how else are you going to *make* them do what you want?

The drive to bend children to our will runs very deep. All parents have, at one time or another, felt that cold hard fury of "Godammit, you'll do as I say!" And the impulse to strike someone who's thwarting our will or making life difficult for us is a perfectly human reaction. When my older daughter, Martha, was about three, she did something that made me furious, and I slapped her. I felt terrible, apologized right away, and she forgave me. Should I have been hauled down to the police station? Of course not. No one suggests that every incidence of spanking should be treated criminally, that behavior arising from the day-to-day frustrations of parenting is on a par with acts of brutality and premeditated abuse. At the same time, declaring something illegal is one powerful way of expressing social disapproval. It's like the difference between committing a hate crime and making a racist joke: the former calls for criminal prosecution, the latter for social disapproval. They're not equivalent, but they do occupy different places on the same continuum of behavior.

In recent years, a number of European countries have outlawed corporal punishment. But in North America, the typical response to such a scenario is along the lines of, "The government can't tell me what I can do in my own home." And indeed, the spanking debate is really about an attempt to re-assert the old parental power structure. But as the wall that traditionally surrounded childhood has fallen away, the power balance between adults and children has shifted dramatically. There is no going back. Children are more autonomous, and parents are no longer able to mold and shape their children in their image, or to screen out the values of the outside world. Toward the end of the nineties, in fact, the whole role of parents in children's lives began to be called into question.

Parents, Peers and the First Three Years

Permissive or strict? Rigid or flexible? Spanking or time-out? Child-centered or good old-fashioned discipline? Or, the most unnerving thought of all: What if none of it really matters?

In the past few years, new voices that challenge the whole orthodoxy of the parenting establishment have joined the debate. These critics are advancing the heretical notion that how kids are raised may have little to do with how they eventually turn out. Judith Rich Harris makes precisely that claim in her controversial 1998 book, *The Nurture Assumption.* Harris argues that the very foundation of most child-development theory rests on an unproven hypothesis that has nevertheless become an article of faith in the field. She marshals an impressive array of evidence to back up her argument that parents may not be all that important in shaping a child's future, including a number of long-term studies of twins raised apart and adoptees raised in the same families. Taken together, these studies suggest that genetics is the chief determinant of personality and IQ in children, and that the importance of the home environment is minimal in comparison. Harris also cites some intriguing research on how kids' behavior is influenced by their peers, which suggests that parents' belief that they are molding and shaping their children's character may be illusory.

Harris doesn't confine herself to questions of science, but weaves her own experiences into the discussion. She recounts how, as a graduate student in her twenties, she was kicked out of the psychology department at Harvard and subsequently made her living by writing and editing child-psychology textbooks. She readily admits that her own outsider status played a key role in shaping her perspective in *The Nurture Assumption,* and indeed much of the book comes across as an attempt to skewer the establishment that shunned her. Harris also makes much of the fact that, despite having been raised in the same household, her own two daughters turned out quite differently. But this point doesn't exactly bolster her case, since many parents talk about how different their children are from one another.

The Nurture Assumption draws on the work of William Corsaro, whose book, *The Sociology of Childhood,* documents his extensive studies of children's peer cultures. Corsaro is one of the few academics who views children as active agents in their own lives rather than as passive products of their upbringing, their genes or the media. But because he's a sociologist and concentrates his research on the world outside the home — where parents are fairly unimportant — his work has been largely ignored by the child-development establishment. Corsaro's work is based on detailed observation of children's actual behavior. He's spent many hours with kids in their own social environments — schools and day-care centers — watching how they form their own mini-societies, establish pecking orders and create imaginative reconstructions of what they see in the adult world. Corsaro believes that children have their own culture (a conclusion I arrived at — by admittedly less rigorous means — in my earlier book *Kid Culture*). His work lends weight to Harris's most radical and contentious claim: namely, that peer-groups are far more important than parents in raising children and shaping their personalities.

Another critic of prevailing orthodoxies is John Bruer, whose *The Myth of the First Three Years* challenges the notion of a critical period in early childhood for healthy intellectual and emotional development. According to Bruer, the idea that the brain is mostly hardwired by the age of three has become popular, but is largely unproven. Bruer cites recent research showing that the brain continues to develop right through puberty, for example, and charges that advocates have overstated the case for the importance of the first three years, unnecessarily frightening parents into believing that it's game over if their kids don't get everything they need in the first few years.

To outsiders, internecine professional squabbles can be utterly mystifying, like medieval debates about how many angels can dance on the head of a pin. They often make me want to interrupt, like the announcer in the old Certs breath mint commercial, and shout, "Stop! You're both right!" I think ordinary people understand perfectly well that the forces that shape children are complex, that parenting isn't really an either-or proposition. Common sense tells us that what happens to babies in their earliest years *is* important, that parents matter more in infancy, while peers grow in importance as children move into the world outside the home. But arcane as these debates may seem, they're still significant in the way they express aspects of our collective view of children, and they do have real-world repercussions. For example, though I tend to agree with Bruer's view that the importance of the first three years has been oversold, I'm concerned that his book offers tight-fisted governments a ready-made excuse for not supporting early-childhood programs.

To me, there's an underlying problem in this whole debate, and it has to do with our culture's overemphasis on the way kids turn out. For most grown-ups, childhood is little more than a way station on the road to adulthood: we're keenly interested in kids' futures ("What do you want to be when you grow up?"), but not nearly as interested in what they're like right now. For instance, Early Childhood Education advocates know they won't get very far arguing for programs simply to make kids' lives better in the present. So instead they talk about such programs as an "investment in the future" that will result in better academic performance and career success.

The views of Harris, Corsaro and Bruer offer a necessary corrective to some of the current child-rearing orthodoxies, and raise some questions that need to be talked about. At the very least, they suggest that maybe parents should stop trying so hard to be perfect. Even the experts say things are getting out of hand; some of them view this collective obsession with parenting as a new kind of dysfunction, a syndrome variously named (depending on which book you consult) over-parenting or hyper-parenting. When the subject was first raised in 2000, the media pounced on some particularly meaty examples: the father who offered to pay his child's nanny an extra $500 for every developmental milestone the kid reached while in her care; parents who sought therapy for their thirteen-year-old son because they were worried he lacked the "killer instinct" for success. Another manifestation is some parents' over-vigilance and obsessive concerns about safety, which leads to what has to be the sorriest trend of all: the video monitoring of nannies.

Most people don't resort to these kinds of measures. But still, the rest of us garden-variety parents agonize: Are we doing it right? Are we doing *enough*? In earlier historical periods, families worried about passing on a sufficient inheritance to their children. This striving to give kids every advantage is the modern-day version of patrimony. For example, summer camp in the great outdoors just doesn't cut it with many of today's parents, who are packing kids off to computer camps instead. Tutoring centers report that the summer break is their equivalent of the Christmas rush. These aren't just for kids who are falling behind and need extra help. By far the greater proportion of students are the offspring of middle-class parents who want to give their kids an edge. Even birthday parties are becoming opportunities for self-improvement. Tutoring centers have begun to offer all-inclusive party packages, with computer games, math brush-up sessions, and loot bags filled with pencils and erasers instead of the usual cheap plastic trinkets. (Mind you, there's still candy and cake, though staff have reportedly complained about having to clean crumbs out of the keyboards.) Pay-and-play centers, which are cropping up all over North America, are another part of this trend. Instead of going to the local playground or — horrors — letting kids run free around the neighborhood, parents are taking them to these indoor theme parks, with a selection of computer games and high-tech toys that puts ordinary households to shame.

Meanwhile, many child-development professionals report that

kids' lives are over-programmed, and that increasing numbers of them are suffering from a form of burnout. All this parenting, it turns out, may be hazardous to kids' health. And if it isn't enough that parents have their own insecurities to contend with, they also have to deal with a society that can be downright hostile to their predicament.

The Home vs. The World

All that New Yorker Gail Bryce wanted to do was to sit and sip her café latte in peace. It was bad enough that legions of baby strollers were crowding the streets of her Upper West Side neighborhood. Bad enough too that she had to put up with small children robbing her of a seat on the subway, even though they were riding for free and she was a fare-paying customer. But when her local Starbucks was overrun with little kids climbing on the windowsills, running about and — worst of all — *staring* at her, Bryce decided she'd had enough. She didn't just stew about it. She went home and wrote a full-page rant for the community newspaper. Bryce's piece in the *West Side Spirit*, "Your Kids are Driving Me Crazy," touched off an urban firestorm. The paper received a flood of mail from other beleaguered New Yorkers, many of whom applauded the author for daring to say out loud what they were thinking. "I raise my cappuccino to Gail Bryce," said one, "for speaking up for those who respect civility."

To those who didn't live in Upper West Side Manhattan, the whole flap seemed like little more than a tempest in a latte mug. But the impassioned response to Bryce's article is indicative of a deeper current of resentment against people with children, one that can be summed up in one phrase: *"Your* kids aren't *my* problem." This anti-child attitude forms part of the root of the tax revolt that's swept Western governments over the past decade, as people voice sentiments like "I don't see why my taxes should go to pay for other people's kids." In some quarters, people without children even object to having a portion of their taxes go to pay for public education.

While not everyone takes it to this extreme, these ideas have come to be seen as normal. In our culture, having children is viewed as a purely personal undertaking, a lifestyle choice. The idea that, in bearing and rearing children, parents are taking on a larger social task — one vital to the well-being of society as a whole — has little currency. We've come to view the family as an island unto itself, with sole financial, moral and social responsibility for child rearing. But in this, we're the oddballs.

In the great sweep of history, our view of the family is one peculiar notion indeed. We still hold up the nuclear family — consisting of two parents of the opposite sex and their biological children — as the ideal. But where does this leave single-parents, blended families, gay parents and any number of child-rearing arrangements that don't conform to this model? In fact, this idealized version of the family is itself a historical anomaly — the exception rather than the rule.

The family as it exists in the developed world could not exist without the notion of private life. But the idea of privacy is a relatively recent development; the distinction between private and public life was unknown until about 300 years ago. Prior to that, even middle-class families lived a kind of fishbowl existence. Their large houses were bustling with servants, relatives, employees and various hangers-on who might drop by at any time. Up until the end of the 17th century, solitude was an almost unknown experience. In the 18th century, the layouts of houses began to change, along with the social interactions that took place in them. Families began to create a zone of private life, one that expanded over the next few centuries. The multi-generational character of these families began to change as well, moving closer to the nuclear family we know today. The result is, as Philippe Ariès says, that the modern family "cuts itself off from the world and opposes to society the isolated group of parents and children."[2] In simpler terms, it's us-against-them, the home vs. the world.

The rise of Freudian psychology in the 19th century furthered this separation of the nuclear family from the larger community. Freud zeroed in on the parent-child bond — which he saw as the primary force in shaping personality — and proposed what was, in his day, a radically new idea: that what transpires between parents and children in the first few years has enormous consequences that resonate throughout life. In Freud's scheme, the family was a seething cauldron of unexpressed wishes and powerful emotions. With its intense focus on the psychodrama within the household, Freudianism encouraged the already apparent tendency of the family to turn inward, to become less connected to and concerned with the world beyond the household.

Yet even some of Freud's own adherents, like the pioneering anthropologist Margaret Mead, questioned whether the kind of emotional traumas he had found so prevalent in the 19th century European bourgeois family were universal in human societies. When Mead first undertook her study of Samoans in the twenties, she documented quite a different family dynamic, one in which the parent-child bond was not nearly as fraught with emotion as in the West. Mead described child rearing in Samoa as a composite affair, in which biological parents were only part of the mix of influences children were exposed to. In Samoan households, older siblings and other members of the extended family played just as important a role. "Children reared in households where there are a half dozen adult women to care for them and dry their tears, and a half dozen adult males, all of whom represent constituted authority," Mead observed "do not distinguish their parents as sharply as our children do."[3]

Many of the world's cultures share this looser idea of what is and is not family. Many North American native groups, for instance, practice a type of informal adoption in which children can go live with relatives or neighbors if they aren't getting along with their parents, or if there are other difficulties in the household. While the parent-child bond is considered important, it doesn't have the exclusive, overriding importance that we give it. Many cultures lack the hovering quality of our style of parenting; children essentially raise themselves by absorbing and observing what's around them, while the adults watch from a distance, mainly to make sure they're safe and fed.

There was a brief period during the sixties and early seventies when leftists and feminists offered up a stinging critique of the nuclear family. These people were influenced by radical theorists like R.D. Laing and David Cooper, two British psychologists who regarded the family as a toxic institution and an instrument of oppression. These views inspired a period of social experimentation and activism meant to break away from that oppression. Adults lived in communes where they tried raising children co-operatively. Much of the extensive child-care system we have today is a direct result of the efforts of those pioneering day-care parents. Of course there was much that was misguided about those times, too; when I look back at the rhetoric of the period (including my own), a lot of it appears faintly ridiculous now. But at the core is an idea that I think we have yet to come to grips with. By acknowledging that children benefit from contact with an array of other adults, other children and other influences, the radicals of the sixties and seventies affirmed their belief that the family should not be a closed system, and that children are members of the larger community right from birth.

One reason for the overwhelming insecurity parents feel these days — and why they've become so dependent on the glut of parenting books — may be precisely because the pendulum has swung too far in one direction. Parents are expected (and expect themselves) to do an impossible job, to single-handedly serve as the "haven in a heartless world" (to borrow from the title of Christopher Lasch's 1977 book on the family). But just as the walls around childhood are tumbling down, the walls isolating the family are crumbling too. Kids aren't being molded exclusively by parents anymore. For better or for worse, the values of the larger culture are seeping into the family, and increasingly, the reach of that culture is a global one.

NOTES

1. John Rosemond, *To Spank or Not to Spank: A Parents' Handbook* (Kansas City, MO: Andrews and McMeel, 1994), 46.
2. Philippe Ariès, *Centuries of Childhood,* translated from the French by Robert Baldick. (New York: Vintage Books, 1962), 405.
3. Margaret Mead, *Coming of Age in Samoa* (New York: William Morrow and Co., 1928), 209.

IT TAKES A (GLOBAL) VILLAGE

N THE SPRING OF 1998, Ivy and I were invited to take part in an
international conference on children's television held in London,
England. Ivy served as one of the Junior Delegates, a group of
kids from all over the world who were there to draft an international Children's Television Charter and to give some street cred, as it
were, to the proceedings. (For her pains, Ivy got free lunches hosted
by McDonald's and the Rainforest Café, T-shirts, backpacks and a
whole slew of other items emblazoned with the logos of various corporate sponsors.)

For my part, I split my time between serving as one of the
leaders of the kids' workshops, and attending panels and speeches by
academics, producers and various other grown-ups. There were some
fascinating discussions; this was the same symposium I mentioned
back in Chapter Five, where the *Teletubbies* controversy first ignited.
But I found the Junior Delegates' workshops even more interesting
— not to mention more fun. At first they were fairly shy about speaking out, and careful to say what they thought the adults wanted to
hear. But as the week wore on, they grew more vocal and forthright in
their opinions. At one point, the kids in my group said they were a
bit tired of always hearing adults talk about how bad television was.
For a change, they wanted to talk about what they *liked* about television. They decided to go around the circle and name their favorite
TV shows and why they liked them.

Almost without exception, they named shows produced in their home countries: a kids' show produced by a Gaelic-language station in Scotland; an animated cartoon made in South Africa; a fascinating array of other shows I'd never heard of and will likely never have the opportunity to see. At the same time, most of the kids felt they wanted to name more than one show, and in almost every case their second choice was *The Simpsons*. It was an intriguing juxtaposition. Clearly these were kids who knew where they came from and were proud of their own culture. At the same time, children from war-torn Bosnia to the affluent suburbs of Colorado watched and loved this animated sitcom about a bumbling, blue-collar American and his family. The shows made in their home countries distinguished the delegates from one another, but *The Simpsons* was a glue that bound them together, across linguistic and national boundaries.

In a world where cable TV and satellite dishes have penetrated the slums of New Delhi and the *barrios* of Latin America — where MTV is broadcast in more than eighty countries — it's no exaggeration to say that most kids are growing up with a common global culture. They watch the same movies and TV shows, play the same computer games, listen to much of the same music and covet the same fashions. Who's raising the kids? Increasingly, the answer is global popular culture.

Crud Culture

By no means does everyone think this global youth culture is so great. Many people cheered when writer David Denby called it "an avalanche of crud" in a much-discussed *New Yorker* piece in 1996. Observing the tastes of his own children and their friends, Denby concluded that in a culture where the media are all-pervasive, kids today are growing up in a "degraded environment that devalues everything."[1] From this point of view, the problem isn't just that the media universe is ridden with sex, violence, and commercialism, but that it's lowbrow, crude and vulgar (come to think of it, kind of like Homer Simpson himself). Denby's piece puts him squarely in the camp of the cultural pessimists — people who believe (and cling determinedly to the belief) that society is in a state of irreversible cultural decline. Perhaps the most tenacious manifestation of this kind of pessimism is found in our widespread contempt for television — not just for the content of its programming, but for the *medium*. There's no lack of people who proclaim in tones of moral superiority that they hardly ever watch TV, or don't even own one. Still, there are plenty of others out there spending time in front of what many fondly refer to as the boob tube.

One of the main objections to kids spending so much time with screen-based media is the conviction that these undermine literacy and destroy the imagination. It seems clear that we're in the midst of a historical shift, in which the image is gaining ascendancy while the written word is declining in importance. Whether this means the decline of civilization itself, is, however, debatable. As for the concerns about children's imagination, the argument that's usually trotted out is that reading is superior because children must supply the pictures in their heads, while seeing images leaves nothing to the imagination. But I've never been all that convinced of it. I doubt very much whether child-development experts and social-science researchers have a better handle on how the imagination works than the artists and writers who have to use it all the time. (Many of them even work in television.)

Much of the power of the image stems from its exportability. Information in visual form is available to people with low levels of literacy, and many of the world's cultures value the image more than the West does. In truth, there's no resisting the tide of global pop culture. As the Junior Delegates at the TV conference made clear, kids are already growing up in it. We can dismiss it all as crud and say the world's going to hell in a handbasket, as the cultural pessimists do. But we'll be far more help to kids if we put aside our blanket condemnations, and help them learn to navigate through the stuff. One of the most important developments in this direction is the worldwide movement for media education. By helping kids to see the messages they're getting and to understand the mechanisms by which they're transmitted, media educators help demystify the media for them. In this way kids can learn to discriminate, in the positive sense of the word.

A groundbreaking demonstration of how TV and global culture can be a force for good is that old favorite, *Sesame Street*. For North Americans, the show has long passed into the pop culture pantheon as a great piece of all-ages entertainment. But on a worldwide scale, *Sesame Street* has moved into another dimension altogether. In what can be seen as a more enlightened version of the corporate concept of branding, the producers of *Sesame Street* have for the past decade been branching out all over the globe, homegrown versions of the show have been developed in more than 120 countries, including Russia and China. These aren't the typical dubbed versions made by most American TV shows; as much as possible, they're produced locally. A particular emphasis is made to promote peace in areas where children have suffered the effects of war and ethnic strife. The most remarkable success has been the Arab–Israeli co-production known in Hebrew as *Rechov Sumsum* and as *Sharaa Simsim* in Arabic. First broadcast in 1998, the show has characters from both groups, but there's no pretense that everyone lives happily together. Instead, it shows them living separate lives on separate streets, speaking their own respective languages, and visiting one another in crossover segments. Both shows attempt to break down negative stereotypes of the enemy, and try to foster the notion that a child from an "enemy" group can be a potential friend. Surveys show that the program at least partially achieves its aim — children in both groups who had watched the program for a few months had more positive views of people on the other side than before they'd started watching it.

The Simpsons and *Sesame Street* are like two poles of global youth culture: the former is one-size-fits-all, the other locally produced in varying forms. But what both do is give kids from all over the world a common point of reference. Critics charge that global culture means nothing but jeans, Disney, Coca-Cola and the destruction of indigenous cultures. But it's more complicated than that. Globalization can also mean cultural cross-fertilization, as it has in the world-music scene. There's evidence that the movement of trends and crazes is shifting. Time was when all fads originated in the U.S., but arguably Japan has had almost as great a global cultural influence in recent years, with the proliferation of Pokémon, the cult appeal of anime and even the ubiquitous Hello Kitty. In fact, the turn-of-the-millennium craze for scooters reversed the usual order; it started in Europe, spread east to Japan and Australia, and hit North America last. The world really is growing smaller and, more than any previous generation, today's kids see themselves as citizens of what Marshall McLuhan first termed as the global village more than thirty years ago.

Global Citizens

So ingrained is our cultural pessimism that those who suggest that the upcoming generation is more together than previous ones risk being dismissed as Pollyannas. But there are plenty of indicators to show that this is what's happening. Certainly many kids' awareness of the world far outstrips their predecessors'. When I grew up in the fifties, the starving millions were just an abstraction to me (and certainly not a good reason why I should have to eat my spinach). But now kids watch infomercials about the Third World from the time they can sit upright. Laugh all you want at Sally Struthers and other purveyors of starving-children posters: these ads make a deep impression on kids in Western countries, who immediately perceive the gap between the skinny kids on TV and their own materially comfortable lives. They respond with an instinctive and boundless compassion, and usually want to race right to the phone to make a donation. (This is, of course, where adult judgment comes into play. Little kids would gladly clear out the family nest egg at one go in the mistaken belief that's all it would take to relieve the suffering they see on the screen.)

Many kids also have a comfort with diversity that their elders can only dream of. Of course racism in its many forms is alive and well, but it looks as though a real sea-change is occurring. In urban centers like Toronto, where I live, kids go to multi-racial schools from the time they're toddlers. Friendships can matter-of-factly cross color and cultural lines; interracial dating is generally no big deal. This generation has been called color-blind — not in the sense that they think everyone's the same, but in the sense that they're not as threatened by differences and don't necessarily treat people different from themselves as "the other," the way older people tend to do.

They also have an unprecedented awareness of world issues. Kids today are just as likely to write papers on Third World sweat-shops or biotechnology as on how they spent their summer vacations. Environmentalism is also an overriding concern. For example, young activists were key to the success of a campaign to prevent the whole-sale development of a major watershed in Toronto's environmentally sensitive Rouge Valley. According to the organizers, it was the emotional speeches and presentations by fifteen- and sixteen-year-olds that tipped the balance at several key meetings. Some observers have concluded that kids really are kinder, gentler and more altruistic now, tagging them with labels like "the sunshine generation" and "good scouts." A 1999 survey of 5,000 young people in eleven different countries found that, overall, they had high levels of altruism, were optimistic about the future and tended to be critical of the workaholic lifestyle of many of their parents.

A textbook example of the "good scout" is Craig Keilburger of Thornhill, Ontario. In 1995, at the age of twelve, Keilburger was moved by a newspaper account of the murder of Iqbal Masih, a young Pakistani carpet weaver. When he was twelve, Masih became an activist, protesting against the exploitation of child laborers in Third World countries. It's widely believed his political activities were the reason behind his still-unsolved murder. Keilburger had found his cause, and with some classmates he started an organization called Free the Children to work for a worldwide ban on child labor. Keilburger quickly became a media sensation. He was interviewed on *60 Minutes* and embarked on several international speaking tours to raise awareness about the issue of child labor, and how it tends to be perpetuated within a competitive global economy.

In some ways, Keilburger is typical of the Echo generation. His boomer-era parents were politically active, and his older brother was involved in environmental issues. But few adults had ever encountered a child as articulate as Craig Keilburger, and though his devotion to his cause was at first lauded, a backlash soon began to set in. To many of the jaded media types covering Free the Children, Keilburger was just too goody-goody to believe. It was as if they didn't know what to make of a kid who didn't fit the stereotype of disaffected youth hanging out in shopping malls. Many protested that he should be doing kid (i.e. inconsequential) things instead of campaigning on world issues. In 1998, a major Canadian magazine, *Saturday Night,* carried a stinging profile suggesting Keilburger was a puppet manipulated by ambitious parents. The article also made veiled insinuations that the family was profiting financially from Free the Children's fundraising. Keilburger sued the magazine and won.

The prime impulse behind much of this new activism is a sense of solidarity with young people in other countries. Keilburger's response to the tragedy of Masih's death was a feeling of kinship, coupled with a sense of outrage that led him to take up and continue the fight. Good scouts harbor no illusions; they know they live lives of enormous privilege compared to the vast majority of the world's young people. Throughout this book, I've talked about the erosion of the protective wall of childhood. But the reality is that large numbers of the world's children haven't experienced life in this protected realm. Childhood is a luxury they've never had a chance to lose. They work in sweatshops, grow up in war zones, or are abandoned to fend for themselves on the streets and even underground, as in the case of the much-reported-on sewer children of Mongolia.

Not all of today's young activists are of Keilburger's clean-cut variety. Some are kids with tattoos, piercings, dreadlocks or multi-colored hair, who dress in hip-hop or rave fashions or wear Doc Martens. Their activism takes the form of "culture-jamming" directed against the ever-expanding domination of multinational corporations. Many of these kids prefer spray-painting Nike ads, creating graffiti, performing street theater and making their own music, books and art to traditional forms of political expression. But some of them are also ready to use militant, confrontational tactics when the situation warrants, as the widely reported demonstrations against the World Trade Organization in Seattle and Prague show.

One thing is certain: the new activists are no longer content to let adults set the agenda. In November 1999, UNICEF Canada organized a national election on children's rights, in which partici-pants were given a list of ten rights, including the right to such basic necessities as shelter, health care, and even the right to a family. They were asked to vote on which one was most important to them. Organizers were shocked when the exercise backfired. Various youth groups across the country refused to take part, saying the whole approach to the election demeaned and patronized them. Among the harshest critics was Craig Keilburger, who denounced the election as tokenism and pointed out that adults would never be asked to choose among their basic rights in the same way UNICEF was asking children to do. In rejecting the UNICEF initiative, what these kids were saying was that they wanted *real* participation in the political process. Keilburger, in fact, is part of a growing worldwide movement to lower the legal voting age to sixteen, a measure that's already been adopted in Brazil and is under consideration in several European countries.

There are signs that we're witnessing a profound shift in values similar to that of the late sixties, when many cultural barriers began to fall. But today's kids have a problem the sixties activists didn't have. Like their Gen-X predecessors, they have to contend with boomers telling them, in so many words, "We've already done it; whatever your generation does will just be a pale imitation." But it's not true. As someone who lived through that time, I think the sixties have been mythologized beyond recognition. The whole era is now viewed through a nostalgic lens, much like an edited series of highlights. Just who's to say Seattle won't be remembered as a key turning point in the way the 1968 Democratic convention in Chicago was?

There are already signs that this generation is departing from previous scripts and going beyond the old left-right split. Whatever happens, their "revolution" will be different from the boomers'. Lacking a singular issue such as Vietnam, in a culture where the traditional restraints on sexuality have fallen and where drugs are part of the landscape, the changes wrought by the new generation may not have the same flair as the long-haired freaks smoking pot and carrying signs saying "Make love not war." But in contrast to their parents' generation, there's every chance they'll grow more socially conscious, not less, as they get older. And they have a whole new set of tools to work with. We've already seen the key role the Internet played in the organization of the anti-World Trade Organization demonstrations in Seattle. Given their political sophistication, coupled with their expertise in new communications technology, the Echo generation could well make the sixties look like a tea party in comparison.

Notes

1. David Denby, "Buried Alive: Our Children and the Avalanche of Crud," *The New Yorker* (July 15, 1996), 48.

CONCLUSION

BEYOND OUR COMMAND

Come mothers and fathers
Throughout the land
And don't criticize
What you can't understand
Your sons and daughters
Are beyond your command
Your old road is
Rapidly agin'
Please get out of the new one
If you can't lend your hand
For the times they are a-changin'
— from "The Times They Are A-Changin'" by Bob Dylan

IN THE MID-NINETIES, the Bank of Montreal — one of Canada's major financial institutions — launched a massive ad campaign aimed at re-branding the bank as a forward-looking, visionary company with its finger on the pulse of the new generation. The campaign's slogan was "Can a bank change?" The company even adopted a new name, re-casting itself as the ultra-hip "mbanx". (Turned out there were some things a bank couldn't change, though: the public never took to the new name, and the company soon went back to being plain old Bank of Montreal again.) The main thrust of the campaign was a series of TV spots that featured children laughing, swinging and gamboling in grassy fields — the very vision of hope for the future — while an

174

angelic choir of young voices sang "The Times They Are A-Changin'" in the background.

There were ripples of disappointment and outrage when it became known that Bob Dylan had given a bank permission to use his famous paean to sixties' radicalism in this way. It was interesting that the bank elected not to use the verse quoted at the beginning of this chapter, though, with its evocation of angry, disruptive, rebellious youth. I guess the lyrics didn't convey the mood of sunny optimism the ads were meant to impart. But that penultimate verse of Dylan's sixties' anthem is even truer today than when it was written. Kids today *are* beyond the command of adults in a way they haven't been before. They're no longer confined by the old limitations of the walled garden of childhood. Instead, they freely assert their right to be active agents in their own lives and in the larger culture. It's adults who have to get out of the way; who have to adjust to new ground rules; who have to get used to a whole new way of relating to young people.

Gimme Some Respect

Respect your elders: it's one of the oldest commandments in our culture, an exhortation we've traditionally given to children right from the time they're old enough to understand it. And as a guide to human relations, there's certainly nothing wrong with it. But now, kids are rejecting the notion that adults are entitled to respect simply because they're older. In their eyes, respect is a two-way street, a mutual relationship based on a person's worth as a human being — something that has nothing to do with age. When I was growing up, my teachers, my friends' parents and the owner of the corner drugstore were all addressed as Mr., Miss or Mrs. Before the seventies, it was almost unheard-of for a child to call a grown-up by his or her first name. Nowadays, it's commonplace, but a good many adults aren't comfortable with the new order. People still write to Ann Landers and

Miss Manners complaining about the practice, arguing that adults should be addressed properly as a mark of respect. But these formalities mean no such thing. They have absolutely no bearing on whether a child actually regards a particular person with respect.

It's not hard to find examples to point to: one of my daughter's former teachers, for instance, was quite comfortable with her students calling her by her first name. This particular teacher was strict and demanding, but also enormously well-liked. "Everybody respects Gayle," Ivy would often tell me. But it never would have occurred to her that calling a teacher by her first name in any way diminished that high level of respect. This teacher is a good example of the kind of natural authority — to use John Holt's phrase — that certain adults have the ability to command. Kids accord these people respect, not simply because they're grown-ups and thus in a position of authority, but because of how they conduct themselves.

Other forms of respect that kids have traditionally been expected to adhere to are falling by the wayside, too. When Nelson Mandela came to Canada on his 1998 world tour, he spoke at a rally of more than 40,000 people — most of them schoolchildren — at Toronto's SkyDome. During Ontario Premier Mike Harris' remarks before Mandela's speech, a prolonged wave of booing echoed through the cavernous SkyDome. At the time, Harris was the target of stinging criticism from many quarters for his government's funding cuts to welfare and education. The spectacle of thousands of kids heckling a provincial premier in front of a world leader of Mandela's stature — on national TV, no less — touched off a heated media debate. People were outraged by such a display of disrespect, which many chalked up to typical pre-adolescent obnoxiousness. "Whatever you think of Mr. Harris," one phone-in show caller thundered, "this was neither the time nor the place to voice your protest." (It's a curious argument, when you consider that Mandela himself spent most of his adult life in prison for protesting against an oppressive political regime.) But others pointed out that, if the kids' booing was just a case of rowdiness, why didn't they heckle any of the other dignitaries, such as Prime Minister Jean Chretien? And students cheered wildly that day for Mandela. They listened with rapt attention to every word of his speech. As much as adults persisted in writing them off as an unruly bunch of goof-offs, the kids at the SkyDome rally knew exactly what they were doing. Their booing of Harris was a political statement.

The End of Protectionism

When author Marie Winn (to whom I referred at the beginning of this book) wrote back in the early eighties that "The Age of Protection has ended. An Age of Preparation has set in," she was more prophetic than she realized.[1] A convergence of forces in modern life — including such factors as television, the Internet and changes in patterns of child rearing — has resulted in the erosion of the wall of enforced ignorance that has surrounded childhood in Western society for the past several hundred years. The original intent behind the erection of this wall was, of course, a protective one. But it's not working anymore. Winn was right. The era of keeping kids in the dark is over.

Not everyone's ready to throw in the towel, of course. Far from it. An extreme form of protectionism, for example, forms the basis of much of the home-schooling movement that's swept across North America in recent years. A large number of the parents involved are right-wing Christians who are taking their children out of public schools in an effort to rigidly control the influences to which they're exposed. There are some perfectly good reasons why parents might opt for home-schooling, but in a lot of cases it's an attempt to re-assert parental authority and to bolster their right to mold their children in their own image. They are reacting to the understanding that, as Neil Postman observes, there's a sense in which all education is inherently subversive: "Any educational project involves in varying degrees, the risk of alienating children from their parents." [2]

While this method of keeping cultural influences at bay can work in the short run, in the long run protectionism is a dead end. It's a war we can't win, because kids no longer accept that adults have the right to control them. But this new relationship between the generations is a trade-off. For what kids lose in no longer being under adult protection, they gain in power over their own lives. In the past women, too, were seen as more delicate, needing special protection and fewer rights. The whole thrust of feminism has been to reject that protected special status and claim the autonomy and power that comes with being treated as an equal.

Still, just as women aren't exactly the same as men, children aren't the same as adults. Feminists argue that there are certain protections that must be retained for women — laws regarding pregnancy leave and the right to control their own fertility, for instance. By the same token, some allowance has to made for the particular realities of being a child. Am I advocating the end to all safeguards for children? Absolutely not. The focus of this book is *cultural* protectionism — the desire to contain and control words, images, music and other mass-produced, creative goods. Many children already have fairly unfettered access to these things; my argument here is that we should stop putting vast amounts of energy into efforts to prevent that access. At the same time, I don't believe we should discard all social and legal protections that have developed over the past couple of centuries for children. Nor should we dismantle our system of universal education and go back to sending children out to work at age seven. I don't think it's at all inconsistent to propose that it's okay to pick and choose those aspects of childhood that adults and kids alike want to keep as part of a special, protected sphere, and those we want to discard.

Not to mention what protections we might want to *add*. There are issues, such as the sexual exploitation of children, in which special protections are not only appropriate but absolutely necessary. Actually instituting these kinds of safeguards has proven very difficult, however. Efforts to combat child prostitution, for example, shed light on the complexities posed by a problem that crosses international borders. After a highly effective crackdown on the child sex trade by the governments of Thailand and other Asian countries in the late nineties, the pedophile tourism industry simply shifted its focus to Latin America. In Costa Rica and Guatemala, street kids as young as nine have recently been found working as prostitutes. And the problem is in no way confined to the developing world. In February of 2001, three people were charged with kidnapping an eleven-year-old Portland, Oregon girl and taking her across the border to Vancouver, British Columbia where she was drugged and forced to work as a child prostitute. Another thorny issue, one which is being profoundly altered by technological change, is the use of children in warfare. With the development of newer, lighter-weight weapons that can be operated by kids as young as ten, growing numbers of children are being drawn into armed conflicts in various hotspots around the globe. The problem of child labor also poses its own particular set of complexities. Opponents of child labor argue, rightly, that young children should be in school instead of working on assembly lines. But what if work follows them right into the classroom? In March, 2001, over forty children were killed in an explosion at an elementary school in rural China. Despite the denials of Chinese authorities, there was little doubt that the blast was caused by explosives the children were handling to make firecrackers, which the school intended to sell to raise money for books and other supplies. In these instances, what's needed is more protection, not less.

A New Pact Between the Generations

Today, nowhere in the world are there elders who know what the children know ... no elders who know what those who have been reared within the last twenty years know about the world into which they were born. [3]

Margaret Mead wrote those words in the seventies, but they are even more relevant to our situation today. Mead is talking about the inability of adults to provide meaningful guidance to the new generation in times of rapid social upheaval. In her book *Culture and Commitment,* she puts forth her view that the generation gap — which was first identified in the sixties —is more than just typical adolescent rebellion or the traditional conflict between young and old. In her view, the sixties marked a historic break with the past and the beginning of a new relationship between the generations. Up until the 20th century, our culture — and indeed most cultures throughout history — was passed on through older people who transmitted knowledge and values to the upcoming generation. In such a society, change happens slowly, if at all, and the young are "taught to replicate the lives of their ancestors." Authority in these cultures resides in the elders, who "create the future by transmitting the past."

Since the sixties, Mead indicates, the generational tables have turned. Rapid technological change and social upheaval have created a situation in which "it is the child — and not the parent or grandparent — who represents what is to come." The problem is that, mentally, we're still operating within the old model, even though it no longer applies. In times like these, according to Mead, it's the adults who have to do much of the changing, growing and adapting, particularly in our willingness to engage in "a continuing dialogue in which the young, free to act on their own initiative, can lead their elders in the direction of the unknown." [4]

Many adults are intimidated by this idea. It feels to them like the natural order of things has been reversed, and kids are now in control. This isn't true, but it's a predictable reaction to a change of this magnitude. The old power relationship between the generations is in the process of dissolving. It is being replaced by something more akin to a pact between equals.

So, what, in this new scheme of things, do adults have to offer? Let me return to the question posed by Neil Postman and quoted in Chapter 1:

What does a forty-year-old have to teach a twelve-year-old if both of them have been seeing the same TV programs, the same movies, the same new shows, listening to the same CDs and calling forth the same information on the Internet?

The answer is — plenty. Just not what we thought. Not those cultural secrets about sex and death that we used to mete out in measured doses. Certainly not much in the way of technological expertise. In many ways, we're even more lost in this brave new world than children are. But it's the very newness of so much around us — the rapid rate of change that kids are living through also — that makes adults' life experience indispensable. In *Culture and Commitment,* Mead stresses that hope for the future must be rooted in memory of the past. This is one thing adults can give young people: memories of a time we have lived through, and a sense of perspective that comes from first-hand knowledge of that time. We may not be able to teach them anything about computers, but we do have wisdom that can only be gained from experience.

The truth is, kids are hungry for adult involvement and guidance — even if they act like they'd sooner die than admit it. But the kind of wisdom they're looking for can be tricky to pass on. Usually, it involves far more listening than it does transmitting information or giving advice. Sometimes it requires that we simply *be* there, up close or off in the background. Whatever we do, if we want to be truly helpful, we have to give up any illusions we might still have of our own omnipotence, because there's simply too much we don't know. Our culture is going through rapid and volatile changes: we can't predict the future, and can't pretend to know what's best for the people who will inhabit it.

Kids are growing up in a virtual global village, but to thrive they also need real, tangible communities, where they can have contact with a whole range of adults who know them and care about them. This kind of community still exists in pockets around the world. Another example to draw from is the medieval village, with its lack of boundaries between families, and between the generations. In this model, the nuclear family reverts back to its older form, the extended family. But now we can embrace not only blood relatives, but any number of people, especially adults who don't have children of their own, but who want to form supportive bonds with the young. This new-yet-old version of the village also offers the possibility for a return to the traditional place of respect for elders, too many of whom are warehoused and made to feel useless in our culture.

This is the point in books like this where the author typically starts to lay out a laundry list of prescriptions. And though there are certainly concrete things that need to be done, I think the real challenge posed by the new reality of childhood is a demand for a shift in attitudes, a need to keep expanding our ideas of what's possible between adults and young people. This is something I keep grappling with myself.

For example, much as I believe in the theory of Letting Kids Do Stuff, in practice I'm a control freak. I can't help it. I hover. As Ivy unfailingly points out whenever she tries to make something in the kitchen, "You're not letting me do it!" So I confess I was a bit skeptical when I heard about the children's work party being organized for a community building project a few months ago. For some time, Toronto Islanders had been involved in renovating a derelict building known as the Shaw House to create a co-operative residence for some of the Island's senior citizens. The bulk of the work was being done by volunteer crews working on weekends. For one of these weekends, my good friends Peter Freeman and Maura McIntyre decided to organize a work party specifically for kids. Their plan was that the kids would not only serve food and run errands, but also get some on-the-job training in the real work of house construction. I didn't attend the work party myself, but Ivy did, and reports came back that she was a concrete leveller *par excellence* — yet another talent I didn't know she had. As I write, the Shaw House is nearing completion. The kids who worked on the crew that weekend can point to the very spots where they dug, filled, pounded and levelled. And I have nothing but admiration for people like Peter and Maura, who talk the talk *and* walk the walk.

Another Island project proved, for me at least, to be a truly mind-altering experience in relations between the generations. In the summer of 2000, more than eighty members of the community were involved in staging a large outdoor theatrical production called *Right of Passage*. The theme of the show was the journey through childhood and adolescence, and it employed music, dance, stiltwalking, masks, and shadowplay — the signature techniques of Shadowland Theatre, the island-based company that produced it. I was involved in a number of capacities — as writer, fundraiser and performer. We worked with a group of island kids for over two years, developing ideas for the show and honing their performing skills. Throughout that time the adults on the project continually struggled with the dilemma of how much to lead the kids and how much to follow their lead. As *Right of Passage* evolved over the course of those two years, we watched many of the kids go through their own passage from childhood to adolescence.

Finally, the show was on its feet. Every evening before the performance, the younger kids, who played angels in the opening scene, would get strapped into their stilts — a process that, as if by magic, transformed them into beings as tall, if not taller, than the adults around them. Meanwhile, the rest of the cast would sit on the lawn beside the community clubhouse, listening to notes from the play's director, Anne Barber. On one of those nights it struck me that Anne, in her role as director, was the embodiment of the natural authority that John Holt talked about. Not because she was a grown-up, but because she knew her stuff and she understood how to lead and inspire us. When there was a problem, she'd listen to what everyone had to say, then make a judgement call regarding what to do about it. To pull off that show we needed leadership, and Anne had the goods, so we — the adults and young people — mutually agreed to invest that authority in her.

On those nights I felt the exhilaration of watching barriers crumble. There we were: kids, teens, grown-ups, tech people, musicians, designers, performers — a group that spanned in age from under six to over sixty. All of us working together in this huge, creative undertaking, trying to figure out how to make each show a bit better than the one before. I realized that, on some level, this was exactly what the show itself was about: the struggle to create a society in which age doesn't matter all that much, because we're all in this together.

At some point, most of us — parents and non-parents alike — have been involved in something where we've felt that cross-generational kinship. But then it's over, we forget about it, and we put our adult hats back on. Do as I say. Don't talk like that. Because I said so.

But that won't wash anymore. Kids want respect. They want to be useful. And they *do* want to learn what we have to teach them. But they don't want to be shunted into some rarified world of their own. They want to take part in the full life of the human community.

∗ ∗ ∗

"Kids are growing up too fast." In this book I've tried to explore the truth of that widespread belief, as well as the roots of the fear that underlies it. It's clear that we're living in the midst of a major historical shift. The protective wall that surrounded childhood for the past few hundred years is rapidly crumbling. As they grow up watching the TV House of Total Disclosure and roaming the wide open frontier of the Internet, children today are seeing, hearing and doing things that used to be the exclusive province of adults. The traditional ways of distinguishing between age groups are disappearing too: In the year 2000, fifty-year-olds read the Harry Potter books, a fifteen-year-old made nearly a million dollars trading stocks on the Internet, seven-year-olds went for beauty makeovers, and people of all ages bought the Beatles' greatest-hits compilation *1*, making it the best-selling CD of the year. We are evolving into a society without clear age distinctions or generational markers.

For many, this new world is profoundly discomfiting. We prefer to look back with nostalgia to a simpler, *Father Knows Best* era. We do this because we're convinced, along with Neil Postman, that the disappearance of the separate realm of childhood has been nothing less than an unmitigated disaster. The whole thrust of this book has been a call to step back from that belief, to pause and consider the possibility that, quite simply, it might not be true.

Of course, something's always lost in times of change and social upheaval. But at the core of our anxieties is the fear that we're losing something particularly precious: innocence, the essential goodness of childhood itself. But I think there's a fundamental confusion here between innocence and ignorance. We believe that maintaining children in a state of innocence depends on our ability to deny them knowledge of certain things — sex, death, the pain of living. But is this really true? Our attempts in that direction certainly haven't amounted to much. From the time they hear their first dirty words, kids have always tried their damndest to uncover the secrets of sex. Children who witness abuse in their own families, live in war zones or fight in armed conflicts already have plenty of acquaintance with violence and death. Even children who live sheltered, stable lives have a hunger to confront and experience the darker side of life, as the endurance of the fairy tale tradition tells us.

To me, the deeper problem with this view of childhood innocence lies in the way it emphasizes the narrow definition of the word as "the state of being unacquainted with evil." I prefer to think of innocence in the broader sense I discussed earlier in this book, which encompasses many other qualities we associate with childhood: simplicity, optimism, openness to new ideas, honesty, emotional directness. Are children losing these qualities along with their ignorance of the world? I would passionately argue that this is not the case.

A journalist observed to me recently that a steady diet of shows like *The Simpsons* is making kids glib and jaded. "Don't you worry," she asked, "that we're producing a generation of cynics?" Her question got me thinking, and I checked my Oxford English Dictionary, which defines a cynic as "a person disposed to rail or find fault ... one who shows a disposition to disbelieve in the sincerity or goodness of human motives and actions, and is wont to express this by sneers and sarcasm." Now, it's certainly true that *The Simpsons* has more of an edge than, say, the average Saturday morning cartoon. But far from turning kids into cynics, I think it feeds their hunger for what's real and authentic. *The Simpsons* is an example of true satire, in that it doles out ridicule not for its own sake, but with an underlying moral purpose. The satirical impulse, which is to expose folly in order that it can be corrected, is rooted not in cynicism, but in the hope that things can be made better than they are.

Our nostalgic attachment to the childhood of the past tends to blind us to what's positive about childhood in the present. Their greater knowledge of the larger world gives children more power over their own lives. They don't have to submit unquestioningly to abuse by adults. They're no longer isolated within the family, which means they have access to other ideas and points of view than the ones they grow up with. They've got a whole new level of comfort with differences between people, and they're developing a truly global consciousness.

Still, in most of the fundamentals, kids today are the same as they've always been. They embrace change rather than fear it. They have boundless curiosity, and aren't weighted down by the need to cling to old ways of doing things. They want to be told the truth. They want to be treated with respect. They want the adults in their lives to be authentic human beings who mean what they say and say what they mean. They want the world to be a better place and they honestly believe that such a thing is possible. Meanwhile, many adults continue to insist that the world's going to hell, that things are worse than ever. We relentlessly communicate to young people the sense that we have all but given up on their entire generation. In light of this widespread loss of faith in the future, I respectfully suggest that it's adults who are the real cynics.

But we can't and mustn't give up. Rather, we have to try and become the kind of grown-ups kids need us to be, particularly when they're navigating the difficult passage through adolescence. This doesn't necessarily mean more, or even better, parenting. In fact, the intense, high-stakes game that child rearing has become in much of the developed world is something we need far less of. Instead, we need to look beyond the family, toward strengthening the bonds of community. Children are raised by and in communities. Adolescents are initiated by and into communities.

It is scary, this emerging new relationship between the generations. Many of us are convinced that if we give kids an inch, they'll take a mile. That they'll take over completely, that the very underpinnings of the social order will crumble. A lot of baby boomer parents, frightened by the rapid pace of social and technological change, are reacting to this newfound power of youth in much the same way as their parents' generation did.

Maybe it's time for grown-ups to heed the exhortation in the Dylan lyrics I quoted at the beginning of this chapter: "Please get out of the new [road] if you can't lend your hand." Or, to paraphrase another bit of late sixties' wisdom, maybe we should consider the possibility that if we're not part of the solution, that makes us part of the problem. We can keep fighting the tide and trying to keep kids inside the walled garden of childhood, with ourselves as the gatekeepers. Or we can work with them to try to understand and bravely face the future they're growing into.

We haven't really lost the kids. But the ground rules have changed. They're not under our thumbs anymore, or following obediently a few steps behind us. They're on the same road we are, walking right alongside us.

NOTES

1. Marie Winn, *Children Without Childhood* (New York: Pantheon Books, 1983), 5.
2. Neil Postman, *Building a Bridge to the Eighteenth Century: How the Past Can Improve Our Future* (New York: Alfred A. Knopf, 1999), 160.
3. Margaret Mead, *Culture and Commitment: The New Relationships Between the Generations in the 1970s* (Garden City, NY: Anchor Press/Doubleday, 1978), 75.
4. Ibid., 88.

SELECTED BIBLIOGRAPHY

Aries, Philippe, *Centuries of Childhood.* Translated from the French by Robert Baldick. New York: Vintage Books, 1962.

Armstrong, Alison and Charles Casement, *The Child and the Machine: Why Computers May Put Our Children's Education At Risk.* Toronto: Key Porter Books, 1998.

Boswell, John, *The Kindness of Strangers: The Abandonment of Children in Western Europe from Late Antiquity to the Renaissance.* New York: Random House, 1988.

Bruer, John T., *The Myth of the First Three Years.* New York: Free Press, 1999.

Corsaro, William A., *Sociology of Childhood.* Thousand Oaks, CA: Pine Forge Press, 1997.

De Mause, Lloyd, ed., *The History of Childhood.* New York: The Psychohistory Press, 1974.

Elkind, David, *The Hurried Child: Growing Up Too Fast Too Soon.* Reading, MA: Addison-Wesley Publishing, 1981.

Erikson, Erik H., *Childhood and Society.* New York: W. W. Norton and Co., 1963.

Golden, Mark, *Children and Childhood in Classical Athens.* Baltimore: Johns Hopkins University Press, 1990.

Gordon, Thomas, *P.E.T.: Parent Effectiveness Training.* New York: Peter H. Wyden, Inc., 1970.

Hannawalt, Barbara, *Growing Up in Medieval London.* New York: Oxford University Press, 1993.

Hersch, Patricia, *A Tribe Apart: A Journey into the Heart of American Adolescence.* New York: Ballantine, 1998.

Hine, Thomas, *The Rise and Fall of the American Teenager.* New York: Avon Books, 1999.

Holt, John, *Escape From Childhood: The Needs and Rights of Children.* New York: E.P. Dutton, 1974.

Katz, Jon, *Virtuous Reality: How America Surrendered Discussion of Moral Values to Opportunists, Nitwits and Blockheads like William Bennett.* New York: Random House, 1997.

Greenleaf, Barbara Kaye, *Childhood Through the Ages: A History of Childhood.* New York: McGraw-Hill, 1978.

Kelman, Suanne, *All in the Family: A Cultural History of Family Life.* Toronto: Penguin/Viking, 1998.

Levi, Giovanni, and Jean-Claude Schmitt, eds., *A History of Young People: Ancient and Medieval Rites of Passage.* Cambridge, MA: Harvard University Press, 1997.

Kline, Stephen, *Out of the Garden: Toys, TV and Children's Culture in the Age of Marketing.* London and New York: Verso, 1993.

McDonnell, Kathleen, *Kid Culture: Children and Adults and Popular Culture.* Toronto: Second Story Press, 1994.

Mead, Margaret, and Martha Wolfenstein, eds., *Childhood in Contemporary Cultures.* Chicago: University of Chicago Press, 1955.

—— Margaret, *Coming of Age in Samoa.* New York: William Morrow and Co., 1928.

—— Margaret, *Culture and Commitment: The New Relationships Between the Generations in the 1970s.* Garden City, NY: Anchor Press/Doubleday, 1978.

Medved, Michael and Diane, *Saving Childhood: Protecting Our Children from the National Assault on Innocence.* New York: HarperCollins, 1998.

Meyerowitz, Joshua, *No Sense of Place: The Impact of Electronic Media on Social Behavior.* New York: Oxford University Press, 1985.

Miller, Alice, *For Your Own Good: Hidden Cruelty in Childrearing and the Roots of Violence.* Translated by Hildegarde and Hunter Hannum. New York: Noonday Press, 1990.

—— Alice, *Prisoners of Childhood.* New York: Basic Books, 1981.

Minow, Newton N. and Craig L. Lamay, *Abandoned in the Wasteland: Children, Television and the First Amendment.* New York: Farrar, Straus and Giroux, 1995.

Montagu, Ashley, *Growing Young.* New York: McGraw-Hill, 1981.

Palladino, Grace, *Teenagers: An American History.* New York: Basic Books, 1996.

Postman, Neil, *Building a Bridge to the Eighteenth Century: How the Past Can Improve Our Future.* New York: Alfred A. Knopf, 1999.

———— Neil, *The Disappearance of Childhood.* New York: Delacorte, 1982.

Rosemond, John, *"Because I Said So": 366 Insightful and Thought-Provoking Reflections on Parenting and Family Life.* Kansas City, MO: Andrews and McMeel, 1996.

———— John, *To Spank or Not to Spank: A Parents' Handbook.* Kansas City, MO: Andrews and McMeel, 1994.

Rushkoff, Douglas, *Playing the Future: How Kids' Culture Can Teach Us to Thrive in an Age of Chaos.* New York: HarperCollins, 1996.

Schindler, Norbert, "Guardians of Disorder: Rituals of Youthful Culture at the Dawn of the Modern Age," in *A History of Young People: Ancient and Medieval Rites of Passage,* edited by Giovanni Levi and Jean-Claude Schmitt. Cambridge, MA: Harvard University Press, 1997.

Shahar, Shulamith, *Childhood in the Middle Ages.* London: Routledge, 1990.

Somerville, C. John, *The Rise and Fall of Childhood.* New York: Vintage Books, 1990.

Staples, Terry, *All Pals Together: The Story of Children's Cinema.* Edinburgh: University of Edinburgh Press, 1997.

Stoll, Clifford, *High-Tech Heretic: Why Computers Don't Belong in the Classroom and Other Reflections By a Computer Contrarian.* New York: Doubleday, 1999.

Tapscott, Don, *Growing Up Digital: The Rise of the Net Generation.* New York: McGraw-Hill, 1998.

Turkle, Sherry, *Life on the Screen: Identity in the Age of the Internet.* New York: Simon and Shuster, 1995.

Vincent, Isabel, "The Most Powerful 13-Year-Old in the World," *Saturday Night,* November 1996.

Winn, Marie, *Children Without Childhood.* New York: Pantheon Books, 1983.